YOUR FAITH GUIDE

D0400974

CATCHING GOD'S WAVE
FOR YOUR LIFE

BY JEREMY AND JANNA JONES

YOUR FAITH GUIDE
TO BECOMING A
SOUL SURFER

SOUL
SURFER

CATCHING GOD'S WAVE
FOR YOUR LIFE

BY JEREMY AND JANNA JONES

SOUL SURFER: Catching God's Wave for Your Life
Copyright © 2011 Outreach Publishing

Outreach Inc.
Vista, CA 92081
Outreach.com

All Scripture quotations, unless otherwise indicated, are taken from the Holy Bible, New International Version®, NIV®. Copyright © 1973, 1978, 1984, 2010 by Biblica Inc.™ Used by permission. All rights reserved worldwide. www.zondervan.com

Scripture quotations marked AMP are taken from the Amplified® Bible, Copyright © 1954, 1958, 1962, 1964, 1965, 1987 by The Lockman Foundation. Used by permission. (www.Lockman.org)

Scripture quotations marked NCV are taken from the New Century Version®. Copyright © 2005 by Thomas Nelson, Inc. Used by permission. All rights reserved.

Scripture quotations marked ESV are taken from the Holy Bible, English Standard Version, copyright © 2001 by Crossway Bibles, a division of Good News Publishers. Used by permission. All rights reserved.

Scripture quotations marked MSG are taken from THE MESSAGE, copyright © by Eugene H. Peterson 1993, 1994, 1995, 1996, 2000, 2001, 2002. Used by permission of NavPress Publishing Group.

Scripture quotations marked NLT are taken from The Holy Bible, New Living Translation. Copyright © 1996. Used by permission of Tyndale House Publishers, Incorporated, Wheaton, Illinois 60189. All rights reserved.

Scripture quotations marked NKJV are taken from the New King James Version®. Copyright © 1982 by Thomas Nelson, Inc. Used by permission. All rights reserved.

Scripture quotations marked CEV are from the Contemporary English Version, Copyright © 1991, 1992, 1995 by American Bible Society. Used by permission.

The authors and publisher of this book have sought to locate and secure permission for the inclusion of all copyrighted material in this book. If any such acknowledgments have been inadvertently omitted, the compiler and publisher would appreciate receiving the information so that proper credit may be given in future editions.

ISBN: 978-1-9355-4144-8

Written by Jeremy V. and Janna L. Jones
Edited by Snapdragon Group℠, Tulsa, OK
Cover and Interior Design: Alexia Wuerdeman and Tim Downs

Printed in the United States of America

[God] He reached down from on high and took hold of me; he drew me out of deep waters. He rescued me from my powerful enemy.

Psalm 18:16-17

TABLE OF CONTENTS

INTRODUCTION

This book is based on the message of the movie, *Soul Surfer*, which is the remarkable true story of Bethany Hamilton, who lost her arm in a shark attack, and courageously overcame all odds to become a champion again, inspiring millions worldwide through the love of her family, her sheer determination, and unwavering faith in God. It is filled with inspiring stories and powerful life lessons that will encourage you to discover and pursue the destiny that you have been created for.

So, let's go surfing. You know you want to. The sparkling waves, brilliant sun, and golden sand are all calling your name. Surfers make it look so cool and so easy. They glide across the face of a crystal-blue wave while the sun kisses everything in sight. Ahh, it's like the ultimate this-could-be-you picture.

Well, we're telling you this *could* be you. Don't worry—you don't need a swimsuit, a tan, or even a board. And you don't even have to go to the beach.

Huh?

You can go soul surfing right here, right now.

Hang with us, and you'll discover that soul surfing goes way beyond the water. It's a way of life that takes you on an adventurous ride. It's about hearing a deeper call and diving in with everything you've got. It's about connecting with your Creator, finding your flow, and going for your dreams no matter how calm or stormy the seas of life get. Basically, it's about catching God's wave for your life and riding it with all-out joy.

Sound like something you're up for? Maybe you're ready to jump right in. Or maybe it sounds good but feels scary. That's okay. Start by diving into this book. We'll walk you through the basics of living the life of a soul surfer.

Let's start with who you are and the passions God has placed in your heart. You probably have questions about how to sort out your priorities and purpose. We'll share stories about other soul surfers who have found their way through confusion or conflict to keep following the dreams God gave them.

You'll get to read about what happens when life feels like a Category 5 hurricane blowing everything to bits. You'll meet some soul surfers who endured huge wipeouts—courageous people like Bethany Hamilton.

But we won't leave you hanging, battered by the angry storms. Those will come to an end, and you can find a new perspective.

Are you ready to go for the ride? Are you ready to be a soul surfer? God has big dreams for your life. Dare to trust Him. Let Him take you on the ultimate wave—it's the most exciting and meaningful of all. Dive in and see.

PART 1

The Life of a Soul Surfer

CATCHING GOD'S WAVE

Genesis 1:1–2

In the beginning God created the heavens and the earth. Now the earth was formless and empty, darkness was over the surface of the deep, and the Spirit of God was hovering over the waters.

Psalm 139:13

You created my inmost being; you knit me together in my mother's womb.

Genesis 1:27

God created man in his own image, in the image of God he created him; male and female he created them.

Ephesians 2:10

We are God's workmanship, created in Christ Jesus to do good works, which God prepared in advance for us to do.

Isaiah 43:1

This is what the LORD says—he who created you, O Jacob, he who formed you, O Israel: "Fear not, for I have redeemed you; I have summoned you by name; you are mine."

1 Corinthians 12:4–6

There are different kinds of gifts, but the same Spirit. There are different kinds of service, but the same Lord. There are different kinds of working, but the same God works all of them in all men.

CHAPTER 1
YOU: A SOUL SURFER

"I was born to surf. This is why I wake up at the crack of dawn every day. This is why I endure belly rashes, reef cuts, muscles so tired they feel like noodles."

–Bethany Hamilton in the movie SOUL SURFER

The movie SOUL SURFER introduces us to Bethany Hamilton and her passion for surfing. Even from a young age, all Bethany wanted to do was grab a board and be out in the beauty and power of the Hawaiian waves. When the movie begins, it looks like Bethany's talent and passion are going to take her all the way to a career as a professional surfer.

In this first chapter, you'll read about a crucial point in Bethany's story. You'll read about her amazing inner strength and determination. You'll discover the role faith played in her life and can play in yours also. Read on ...

Halloween turned into a nightmare in a split second. That morning had started beautifully. Most mornings do on the Hawaiian island of Kauai. Young surfer Bethany Hamilton was in her favorite place—the water.

It was barely 6:30 (6:30 a.m.—that's why they call it dawn patrol) when Bethany paddled her surfboard out past the reef. Bethany's best friend, Alana, was with her. Their moms called them mermaids because they grew up together in the water. Alana's dad and brother were there too.

The waves weren't that great, but there was no place Bethany would rather be than in the ocean, especially in the tropical, crystal-clear waters of Kauai.

Surfing can mean a lot of waiting for waves, sometimes. And Bethany and Alana lay on their boards hoping for a swell to appear over the horizon. Bethany dangled her left arm in the water.

That's when it happened. With no warning whatsoever, a fourteen-foot tiger shark burst out of the water. Bethany never saw it coming. She felt a tugging. She saw a huge, bite-shaped section of her surfboard missing. And she saw the water turning red around her. Bethany's arm was gone.

Incredibly, Bethany stayed calm and focused as she started paddling her board for shore with her one good arm. Alana's dad rushed out to meet her. He pushed her board over the reef, tied his shirt around her shoulder like a tourniquet, and had his son call for help.

By the time Bethany arrived at Kauai's only hospital and went into emergency surgery, she had lost about 60 percent of her blood. She was fighting for her life.

Shark attacks almost always make the news, but Bethany's went global. You might remember hearing about it. Maybe the stories get reported because sharks are such scary predators. Maybe Bethany's story got so famous because it seemed so unfair. The victim was a cute, sun-bleached, young teen. The shark was as long as a minivan. Talk about an unfair fight! But probably more compelling was the fact that even with such a ghastly injury, Bethany resisted the urge to panic and paddled herself to shore. She fought for her life and won.

Everyone wanted to hear Bethany's story, and soon she was in major magazines, such as *Sports Illustrated* and *Life*, and on television shows like *20/20*, *Inside Edition*, the *Oprah Winfrey Show*, and *Good Morning America*.

There is hope. There is a foundation strong enough to keep you secure no matter how strong the winds blow. There's a love wide enough to comfort your deepest pain.

All of the attention took Bethany by surprise. She was suddenly a celebrity. But once again, she kept her head. With everyone in the world asking about her miraculous survival, Bethany took every opportunity to credit Jesus for her survival.

But that was just the beginning.

SO HOW'S YOUR LIFE?

Let's get it all out in the open right away.

My life ...

a. rocks. Couldn't be better if I won American Idol tomorrow.

b. is pretty good. My future's so bright that I have to wear shades—most of the time.

c. is okay. So I'm not the king or queen of popularity, but I've got some friends who stick by me on the bad days.

d. is not so good. I feel like I'm going the wrong way on a one-way street.

e. sucks. What good days? I feel like I'm all alone and going under.

Obviously, we'd all like to answer *A*. We'd like for you to be able to answer *A*. But we're not stupid or dreamy enough to think you will. Most of us can't. If you're honest, your answer is probably *F: All of the above*—sometimes all of the above all in one day.

Life is like that. It can especially feel like that during your teen years. Some hours you're on fire; everything's going right. If you were a golfer, you'd be hitting birdies, eagles, or holes-in-one on every hole. If you were a tennis player, you'd be smashing aces. If you were a musician, you'd be receiving standing ovations. Whole days like that are probably rare at best.

But then there are the times when it seems like everything crashes and burns around you. It feels like you're the trailer in the tornado or the bug on the windshield. Those are the kind of days that leave your head spinning and your heart aching. Those are the days that make you question life: What am I good for? Do I really matter? Who am I? And what's the point of it all anyway?

We've all been there. Those days knock you down. They come pouring in like a flood, washing away anything that's not tied down tight. They can strip away everything to the foundation. So what is your foundation? What's your anchor? Is it strong enough to stand?

There is hope. There is a foundation strong enough to keep you secure no matter how strong the winds blow. There's a love wide enough to comfort your deepest pain. There's God's love that never fails or gets blown away by anything.

And God knows a thing or two about bad days and really incredible pain. Jesus has been there and knows exactly how you feel. He walked through hell, literally, for all the evil and sin in the world, including the stuff that's burying you under a landslide of hurt and rejection. He's there with His arms wide open like a friend. He's there like a safety net below your trapeze. And He's there like a rock-solid base to hold you up against all the unfairness of life—no matter what hits you out of the blue.

Maybe you've always known that God loves you. He's been part of your life for as long as you can remember. Or maybe finding out that God wants to be part of your life is news to you. If you've always known Him, this will be one more new and exciting adventure in your life of faith. But if you are just now learning that God loves you and wants to be in your life, say yes to Him. Wonderful discoveries await that will change your life forever. Open your heart and ask Him to come in—don't wait another minute.

SOUL SURFER

The day before Thanksgiving, less than one month after the attack, Bethany surfed again. It took some work to figure out how to balance and push herself to her feet on the board, but she did it. Tears of joy ran down her cheeks. Her family hooted and cheered as Bethany rode the waves again.

Just two months later, Bethany returned to competition surfing at a regional contest. A little while after that, she placed fifth at the National Championship. And the next year, Bethany won the National Championship! Yes, she was the only contestant with one arm, but it didn't slow her down. She was determined to be a pro surfer, and no shark was going to take that dream away from her. No way!

There's one thing you've got to understand about Bethany Hamilton. Surfing was more than something she did—it was her way of life, her passion. Bethany was in the water every day, every chance she got—even at the crack of dawn. She surfed with her parents and her brothers. She surfed with her friends. She surfed alone if she had to. She loved to surf.

Soul surfer has long been the term in surf culture for a person who rides the waves for the pure love and passion of it. Soul surfers don't paddle out only to win big contests and big money. They don't care only about ripping up a wave with the hottest new aerials and tricks. That doesn't mean they can't rip. It just means soul surfers ride the waves for the love of the ocean, no matter who's watching. They know and respect the ocean for everything it offers, not just the playground of waves on its surface but also its life and power deep below the surface. Soul surfers follow the waves for the freedom of the wind and water—not prize money or popularity or fame. They jump on their boards to ride the liquid energy for the sheer adventure of it. And nothing's going to stop them.

Bethany is a soul surfer all the way to her core. But she's even more. She took soul surfing even farther. There is one thing in the world—and only one thing—that Bethany is more passionate about than surfing: Jesus.

It was her relationship with Him that helped her make sense of the tragic shark attack. When Bethany asked, *Why me?* her faith in God led her to the Bible verse *Jeremiah 29:11,* *"I know the plans I have for you," declares the LORD, "plans to prosper you and not to harm you, plans to give you hope and a future."*

She had a hard road to walk and a lot of adjustments to make—try tying your shoe or putting your hair in a ponytail with one hand, or dealing with kids pointing and staring at you. Oh yeah, try paddling a surfboard with one arm and jumping up on it while it's racing down a wave.

But Bethany didn't let self-pity step in and finish what the shark hadn't been able to accomplish. Her

Soul surfer has long been the term in surf culture for a person who rides the waves for the pure love and passion of it.

questions and answers quickly turned to *Why have I been given this opportunity?* Suddenly, the major media of the world came knocking on her door; some of those "plans I have for you" started to make sense. Bethany was able to tell millions of people about Christ's faithfulness to her. She had more attention and recognition than she ever would have had as just another pro surfer. She was an inspiration to the world, and she got to tell the world about the One who is her true inspiration.

Bethany kept her soul surfing truly about soul. She stuck close to Jesus, the lover and Savior of her soul, no matter what. She held on to Him when life imploded. And her passion for God burned through no matter what happened.

> **For soul surfers, love is pure and passion is on fire. They live to swim in God's presence and let God write their stories. They are stoked on God's Spirit. No ocean is required for that.**

YOU TOO

Bethany's doctors call her a living miracle. She is. And so are you. You don't have to survive a shark attack. You don't even have to make it through a terrible car wreck or a life-threatening disease. You're a living miracle because God created you as a special, unique, and amazing individual. You've got a combination of gifts that no one else has, all wrapped into a one-of-a-kind you.

You can be a soul surfer too. Soul surfing goes way beyond Bethany. You can catch God's ultimate wave. You can ride His epic way of life. You can follow His radical adventure. And no, you don't need the ocean. (Although feeling a little sand between your toes every once in a while is nice.)

How do you do it? How does it work? We're going to spend this whole book talking about all that. But here's an overview of where we're headed together. What does it look like to be a soul surfer? A soul surfer...

- believes God created her with potential and promise.

- lives with passion.

- pursues adventure.

- discovers his gifts.

- goes after her dreams.
- puts God first.
- trusts God's good plans even during the wipeouts.
- faces problems with courage.
- overcomes challenges with patience and persistence.
- spreads God's love to other people.
- never gives up.

SOUL SURFING ON THE SHORE

For soul surfers, love is pure and passion is on fire. They live to swim in God's presence and let God write their stories. They are stoked on God's Spirit. No ocean is required for that.

Check out these real-life soul surfers. Not once have they hopped on a board, but they love to flow in God's currents. They move with His tides. They give everything they've got to catch God's wave.

Lauren and Lesley Reavely are teenagers who live in Portland, Oregon. So do a lot of homeless people. The two sisters couldn't help but notice people sleeping under bridges and begging in the rain. They knew Jesus loves everyone, even those who have ended up on the streets. They followed the fire God put in their hearts and started H2O, which stands for Hope 2 Others, by packing and giving out bags of food, basic supplies, and messages of God's hope. Lesley and Lauren are soul surfing a God-sized wave of compassion and service, and it has spread to other cities with new chapters of H2O started by other teens who share the same passion. Along with practical necessities, they are giving away the living water that Jesus was talking about in John 4:13–14 when He said, *"Whoever drinks the water I give him will never thirst. Indeed, the water I give him will become in him a spring of water welling up to eternal life."*

Leeland Moring is crazy about music, always has been. It's what keeps his blood pumping, especially when it's combined with worshipping God. During his teen years, Leeland cut himself off from MTV and got busy spending all his time loving God and playing music that reflected his love. The band that bears his name basically went straight from their youth group to a professional music career. There's nothing better for Leeland and his bandmates than to rock and challenge listeners to live all out, 100 percent passionate for God.

Jamie Tworkowski stumbled into his passion almost by accident—but was it really by accident? No, it was Jamie tuning his heart into the wave God was flowing around him. When Jamie met Renee, she was in the grips of drug addiction, depression, and self-injury. When they couldn't get her into rehab soon enough, Jamie and some other friends stayed with Renee around the clock to help her stay sober. They literally wrote love over the scars on her arms where she had been cutting herself. It was a long process of real love in action, but it connected Renee with God's perfect love. And it led Jamie to start To Write Love on Her Arms, a movement getting help for people with serious pain. God's wave has grown much bigger than Jamie had ever imagined.

WHERE'S YOUR WAVE?

If you've been to the beach, you've probably watched the waves rolling in and crashing on the shore. Did you ever wonder where they come from? Waves are liquid energy that comes from wind. That unseen force blows across the water and starts moving it forward. The stronger the wind, the bigger a swell becomes as it pushes through the ocean until the seafloor gets shallow. Then up goes the water into a wave and whoosh!—it rolls over and breaks, unloading its energy. Sometimes, it's explosive and scary, and sometimes, it's smooth, even, and artistic. Either way, it's awe-inspiring and fun all at the same time. (Remember playing in the waves when you were little? You splashed and dove and tumbled and laughed until you choked on salt water.)

There's nothing better in the world for surfers than riding along in front of all those natural forces coming together at just the right moment. Surfers study weather forecasts; then they drop everything, travel long distances, and sit for hours waiting in the water to be in just the right spot to catch waves.

It's the same kind of dedication soul surfers have catching God's wave. It's His unseen Spirit that works in their lives like the wind. They can't see His power swirling and building and moving His plans forward in and around them, but they can feel it. There's nothing like it in the world. They dedicate themselves to studying God's Word. They wait, listen, and watch the horizon for signs of God's work rolling forward. They want nothing more than to be swept up into the ride of God's love, grace (the undeserved kindness and favor He shows us), and power. There's nothing like it in the universe. It's the ride of a lifetime. Come on and catch it!

YOUR RIDE

Check out some amazing waves. Clark Little is one of the best wave photographers in the world, and you can see his online gallery at ClarkLittlePhotography.com. Look at the different waves—their beauty, power, and uniqueness. The wave God has for each soul surfer who follows Him is unique and full of His power.

Write a prayer to God, letting Him know how you feel about life and about following Him into the wave He has designed for you. Ask Him to guide your journey of becoming a soul surfer.

"You must live in the present, launch yourself on every wave, find your eternity in each moment."
—Henry David Thoreau, author

"Surfing is for life."
—Bruce Jenkins, author

"Soul surfing to me is what you do when you are thoroughly in the moment enjoying and expressing yourself on the wave and being one with the ocean."
—Tom Carroll, Australian surfer

"There's no secret to balance. You just have to feel the waves."
—Frank Herbert, author

CHAPTER 2

YOU: GOD'S MASTERPIECE

"We spent more time wet than we did dry. My mom was convinced we were mermaids."

–Bethany Hamilton in the movie SOUL SURFER

In the movie SOUL SURFER, we first see Bethany Hamilton as a young girl, living in Hawaii and spending most of her time in the water. Although Bethany was born near the ocean, her love for surfing stood out, even in a family of surfers!

Each one of us is born with unique gifts and special interests. Why do you think that is? This chapter will help you answer that question, and at the end of the chapter, we hope you see yourself as a unique, amazing, and greatly loved masterpiece!

Have you ever been to the hospital or a birthing center and looked through the big window into the newborn nursery? It's a pretty amazing sight. Rows of little identical carts lined up with almost-identical-looking babies wrapped in identical blankets wearing identical little pink or blue beanies on their heads. Without the bracelets they wear, those little bundles of joy are hard to tell apart.

It's no wonder newborns sometimes get mixed up at the hospital! (Just kidding! You have the right parents, even though sometimes you might wonder what planet they're from.)

Back to those babies—the truly amazing thing is that under all those identical blankets is a vast collection of unique little individuals—each completely different from the others. Each tiny baby already has its own parents, grandparents, brothers, sisters, and history: how they were conceived, how well they were cared for in the womb, and how they worked their way into the world during delivery. Did they come out quietly or screaming as soon as they saw daylight?

Each little person has a totally unique genetic code, received from both parents but designed by God. Psalm 139:13 says, *"You created my inmost being; you knit me together in my mother's womb."* In other words, no accidents—just miniature miracles of God-designed life.

Looking through that nursery window, there's no way we can ever imagine all that those little lives will experience or accomplish—but God already knows.

Believe it or not, you were once one of those babies. You probably don't remember those days. You were brand-new. Not a blank slate, though. Ephesians 2:10 says you are *"God's workmanship, created in Christ Jesus to do good works, which God prepared in advance for us to do."* That means God designed you to be exactly, precisely, specifically, uniquely, *especially* the way you are. And He knows your story before it's even written.

The adventure of life, then, is yours. It's an adventure of discovering who God made you to be and what that looks like every day. It's a journey of awakening to the things you care about and then living your life in pursuit of those passions.

Remember the first time you tasted ice cream? Or maybe the cake you got on your first birthday—the one you dug into with both fists and smeared all over your face? Your parents probably have

> **The adventure of life, then, is yours. It's an adventure of discovering who God made you to be and what that looks like every day.**

video. But here's the point: One minute you didn't even know cake or ice cream existed; then suddenly you made an awesome discovery. You had an awakening. You tasted the good stuff, and from then on, you wanted more.

Cake and ice cream aren't truly life-changing, but you get the picture. Then again, you could be the next person to change the world with your ice cream or cake. Finding out is all part of the adventure.

Some of those discoveries come suddenly. Some take time. Your family, friends, and location are all part of what shapes you, but they don't define you. They're simply the backdrop for your story. God wants you to work with Him as you write the story of your life.

One thing you will discover more and more is that God is incredibly creative. He made the entire universe that we know and love! If you have a Bible, look at Genesis 1:1–2 (that's the beginning of the first chapter of the first book). It says, "*In the beginning God created the heavens and the earth. Now the earth was formless and empty, darkness was over the surface of the deep, and the Spirit of God was hovering over the waters.*" Think of some of the wonders of the world. Better yet, make a list. We'll get you started, and you can add to it. Think big and think small.

giraffes　＿＿＿＿＿＿＿＿＿＿＿＿＿＿

aurora borealis, you know, the northern lights　＿＿＿＿＿＿＿

black holes　＿＿＿＿＿＿＿＿＿＿＿＿＿

＿＿＿＿＿＿＿＿＿＿＿＿＿＿＿＿＿＿＿＿

＿＿＿＿＿＿＿＿＿＿＿＿＿＿＿＿＿＿＿＿

＿＿＿＿＿＿＿＿＿＿＿＿＿＿＿＿＿＿＿＿

＿＿＿＿＿＿＿＿＿＿＿＿＿＿＿＿＿＿＿＿

That's all stuff God imagined and created. Big stuff like towering mountains and microscopic stuff like a fly's eyeball or the protons and electrons spinning around inside what everything is made of.

Was the human body on your list? Think about this!

- Your lungs contain more than three-hundred-thousand capillaries. If they were all stretched out end to end, they would reach from Los Angeles to Kansas City.

- If your skin was detached from your body, it would weigh nine pounds.

- You already know that no one else in the whole world has the same fingerprints as you, but did you know you also have a unique tongue print?

- Guys, if you never shave or trim your beard, it will grow to about thirty feet long during your lifetime.

- Girls, if you tried to keep all your toenails and fingernails trimmed to a consistent length, you'd have to cut your fingernails a lot more often. They grow four times faster than toenails.

We could write a whole science book about the amazing human body, but you probably already have one of those from biology or physiology class. Doesn't it blow your mind the way God has put you together? Have you ever thought about how many different functions and interactions are going on inside you right now to keep you alive? And that's the thing—you don't have to think about them at all!

God knows all about them, though. He made all of the human stuff for everybody and all of the totally *unique-to-you* details. The Bible says God even knows how many hairs are on your head (see Matthew 10:30). Way to go, God!

PRICELESS ART

Unfortunately, life has a way of making you forget all your miraculous features. Mean words from a friend, a dis from the cool crowd, or embarrassment in front of the whole class seem to erase any wonders of life. They can make you feel like a nobody in a millisecond.

That's when you need to remember that God gave form to the formless and life to the lifeless. He is your

You can't always tell what you're becoming, but God knows. He's continually forming you into the masterpiece He designed.

Creator, and His creative abilities are boundless. And whether you can see it yet or not, you are His masterpiece.

Have you ever watched an artist at work? An artist begins with a glob of clay or a dab of paint. Alone, the medium is nothing artistic or inspiring. It's colorful, maybe, but that's about it. However, in the hands of the artist, it has remarkable potential and promise. There are endless possibilities for what it may become and who it might inspire.

Stick around awhile, and you will begin to see the artist's work take shape. Often, it takes some time to start looking like something special. You may not even be able to tell what it is at first. But the artist knows, and every move of the hand, every stroke of the brush brings it closer to the masterpiece the artist intends.

The same is true for you. You are God's masterpiece. You can't always tell what you're becoming, but God knows. He's continually forming you into the masterpiece He designed.

And when it comes to masterpieces, you're priceless.

YOU CAN'T GROW BEANS FROM RUTABAGA SEEDS

Try looking at it from the world of gardening ...

Spring has sprung. After the long dark days of winter, the sun is shining bright. Jessica walks across the land that will be her summer garden. The ground has thawed after being frozen all winter. Jessica presses her knuckles into the earth. It feels warm. Time to plant. She swings the hoe and forms straight rows. She places the seeds in the ground and covers them with dirt. In the coming days, she'll water them and watch the sun shine down as she waits for her garden to grow.

Suddenly, Jessica realizes she has no idea what kind of seeds she has planted! *Oh well,* she says to herself. *I'll just tell them what to be.* So she makes up songs letting the seeds know what to grow. To the first row, she sings the song of lettuce. To the second row, the song of green beans. To the third and fourth rows, she raps about cucumbers and rutabagas. It's an impressive rap. I mean, you try rhyming—

Hey, wait a minute! It doesn't work like that.

Oh, right. Way to be paying attention. It's ridiculous to think singing a song could make seeds turn into different plants. But that's what we do in life. Instead of spending time looking at how God has made us, we decide what we *should* be and try to convince ourselves to be that. Or we look at what the world around us says is cool and decide *that's* what we're meant to be. But if Jessica planted corn seeds, corn is going to come up out of the ground no matter how many times she sings the green bean song.

Yes, you and I have more choices than a vegetable, and we have the remarkable ability to work and become better at certain tasks and traits. But at our core we are loved by God, designed for His purpose. That's our identity. It's who we are in the deepest places of our hearts and spirits. The more we try to fight it and try to be something else, the more we smack into walls, and the more it hurts.

SHAPING UP

Like art supplies and seeds, surfboards don't look like much when they begin: just big rectangular blocks of polyurethane foam. They get cut into a basic surfboard shape by a computerized machine, but that's not enough to make them ready to ride the waves. They need the touch of the master.

Surfboard shapers are craftsmen and artists. They work carefully with each board to sand its surface and fine-tune every curve. Every millimeter matters in thickness, width, and surface angle. Subtleties that you would never notice jump out like flashing caution lights to an experienced shaper.

John Carper is a famous shaper from Hawaii and a soul surfer in God's sense of the phrase. He also majored in sculpture in college. When he looks at a potential board, he sees it as a future sculpture. And he works with a specific plan in mind.

See, every surfboard has a specific purpose too. Some are meant for beginners and some for experts. Longer boards are built for straighter rides. Shorter boards are designed for lightning-fast turns and tricks. A board built for a thirty-foot wave won't do much good on a thirty-inch wave. That's not its purpose. That wasn't its designer's plan. But put a board into the conditions it was designed for, and it can be like a magic board, flowing just right with the water and waves around it.

God is your master shaper. He's the gardener who planted you specifically. He is the artist who created you as a priceless masterpiece. And once you have invited Him into your heart, your identity as His precious child is secured.

You still might have a million questions about who you are and what you're becoming. That's okay. God's got answers. Keep reading ...

YOUR RIDE

Top surfers decorate their boards with stickers—not just any old stickers but stickers from their sponsors. Those stickers show who they identify with. The stickers say something about their priorities and allegiances.

Who do you represent? Now's your chance to show it. Draw and design your own sticker. Make it your logo. Picture it as something that could go on your surfboard. Use it to show who and what matters to you.

"Jesus invites us on a fascinating, demanding journey. It's a wonder to see where it leads."
—Kent Annan, author of After Shock and co-director of Haiti Partners

"God's gifts put man's best dreams to shame."

—Elizabeth Barrett Browning, poet

"Life is a tapestry: we are the warp; angels, the weft; God, the weaver. Only the Weaver sees the whole design."
—Eileen Elias Freeman, author

CHAPTER 3

YOU: PASSIONATE, GIFTED, CALLED

"I got it all on camera!"

−Noah Hamilton in the movie SOUL SURFER

In the movie SOUL SURFER, *if you watch carefully, you'll see that the members of the Hamilton family have different talents and passions. We know what Bethany loves, but what about her brother Noah? Did you notice in the movie that Noah always seemed to have a camera in his hand? He has had a filmmaking hobby from the time Bethany was a baby. At the end of the movie, the video you see of the real Bethany surfing and as a child were shot by Noah. And guess what Noah does these days? That's right—he's a professional videographer and photographer!*

In chapter 2, we talked about the fact that God made you to be unique and to have a purpose that's different from everyone else's. Maybe you started to think about what your gifts and your purpose might be. In this chapter, we're going to dig a little deeper into that topic.

We don't have all the answers—just wanted to give you that disclaimer up front—sorry, but nobody does. If we did, why would we ever need to use our faith in God?

Following the soul-surfing journey opens up some big questions. You might have some doozies left over from the last chapter: What am I supposed to do? How do I discover who God made me to be? How do I make the right choices?

Those are good questions—important questions. Just because no one else can answer them all for you doesn't mean you shouldn't ask them. God wants you to ask them. He wants you to give your biggest, toughest questions to Him and trust Him. He will answer them and lead you along the way. Just don't expect to see one of those airplanes towing a big banner in the sky with all the answers you ever wanted in life.

That's the attitude of a soul surfer going with God's flow.

God's Spirit gives quieter answers than that. Here's another verse from the Bible: Psalm 119:105 says, *"Your word is a lamp to my feet, and a light for my path."* The Bible, which we call God's Word because it's God's words or letter to us, lights up your next step, not the entire road ahead. No big spotlight is going to light up the details of your *whole* life: Who you will date. Will you make the team? Where you'll go to college. What career you should choose. Who you will marry. Where you will live. How many kids you will have. And how rich you'll be when you retire. God says, "Walk with Me, and let's discover one answer at a time!"

That's the attitude of a soul surfer going with God's flow. It's learning one thing at a time about that masterpiece you were created to be. It's slowly pulling off the wrapping and discovering the gifts and passions God has given you. Yes, you have been given lots of abilities and desires that say a lot about who you are and how God wants to use you. What fun it will be to find out about each one!

THE SETTING

Have you ever read the credits at the end of a movie? All the credits? We know, looooong and booooooring, right? But try it sometime. You'll see names and titles you've never heard of, like gaffers and grips and best boys. Unless you speak Hollywood, it can seem like a different language. But what's important is how many people and how much time and effort go into creating the settings and backdrops of a movie and its story. The way the lights are hung affects the atmosphere and mood of your favorite scene. The costumes and makeup of your favorite characters shape their identities. The location and set bring context and life to the acting. All of those small, surrounding details shape the story.

And guess what? You get to be a star in your own story! Yep, you're the main character, the hero, and the protagonist in the story of your life. That is way cool, but without your setting, you wouldn't have much of a story.

C. J. and Damien Hobgood grew up in Florida. Their parents loved the ocean, and they lived only a five-minute bike ride from the beach. The whole family spent as much time as possible seaside. Is it any surprise that the brothers were riding boogie boards at age four and surfing by the time they were six?

Once they were in school, the Hobgoods would race home after class and get out on the waves as soon as possible. By race, we mean literally racing to beat each other. C. J. and Damien aren't just brothers; they're identical twins. You think it's hard for you to figure out your identity? Try doing it with someone you're always with who looks just like you. Yes, you've got a lot of similarities and people confuse you all the time, but *you* know you're different. You've just got to prove it.

Living in a home near the ocean, being in a family that loved the beach, riding waves every day, being part of a supercompetitive brotherhood, having a twin, and living in a surfing community—those were all part of C. J. and Damien's setting. Their family, location, and the people around them influenced them before the brothers even realized how important it all was. It was just normal life for C. J. and Damien. Only later could they look back and realize how all those factors helped them become two of the best professional surfers in the world.

Most top surfers grow up near the ocean. It makes sense, doesn't it? It's the same reason so many hockey players come from northern places, like Canada, where there's lots of ice. Or why many of the world's best sailors come from Australia, a huge island nation. Our surroundings help shape who we are.

It can be easy to take your setting for granted because it's just there. It's just life.

So how about you? What's the backdrop of your life story? What's your setting? Who plays the supporting roles? Take a look around you. Even if there are not-so-wonderful people or situations in your setting, God can use those to shape you as well, to make you tougher and more compassionate. Nothing is wasted with God, not even your tears.

It can be easy to take your setting for granted because it's just there. It's just life. Fish are no good at telling you about the water—it's just life and atmosphere to them; they don't know anything else. But you're smarter than a fish. You can pay attention. What things, places, experiences, and people have shaped you up to this point in your life? Who do you hang out with? Who do you learn from? Where do you go and spend your time? Watch for rare, big, life-changing events and activities, as well as everyday routines that shape you little by little.

ALL FOR THE LOVE

Richard Rodriguez loves roller coasters. Do you love roller coasters too? Maybe so, but not like this guy. Richard is obsessed. He rode the Pepsi Max Big One at Blackpool Pleasure Beach in England for a record 401 hours in 2007. That's seventeen days straight! It's nearly eight thousand rides, covering more than 6,300 miles. He ate, drank, and slept on the roller coaster with only a mandatory five-minute break every hour. All that riding earned him a world record, and he holds other coaster records as well. Richard is passionate about roller coasters.

What do you really love? What gets you out of bed in the morning (besides an alarm clock)? What do you look forward to? What do you do when you can do anything you want, with no time restrictions? What makes your heart beat faster (besides a special guy or girl)? What gives you extra energy even when you're dead tired? What pumps you up? What gets you amped? What makes you stoked? What gets you geeked?

Start a list. It can be anything at all—pizza, your dog, running, talking on the phone, mission trips, dark chocolate, building stuff, traveling … anything. Don't try to evaluate your list yet. Just write down the things you love.

Next, go back and circle your top three most-favorite, coolest things or activities in the whole world. Those are probably your passions. Those are the ones that drive you. Those are the ones God has put in your heart and connected to the identity and gifts He's created in you. These are a good place to start

GOOD AT THE GIFTS

Meet another soul surfer from the wave-surfing world. Eric Arakawa grew up around surfing, and he loves to ride the waves. He even found out he was good at making, or shaping, surfboards. But after building boards for a while, he started to feel that he should get a "real job." There were doctors, engineers, and teachers in his family, and he felt like he wasn't measuring up. He wanted to accomplish something "more important" than what he was doing.

So Eric started trying to figure out what that something was. That's when he realized something huge. He was really good at building boards. He was gifted. And using those skills was exactly where God wanted him.

Eric started to see a big picture that was so much bigger than just surfboards. He saw where God had placed him in the surf community. He saw the special relationships he had with people around him, including some of the top surfers in the world, and the influence he could have for God just by doing what he was good at. Eric is still building surfboards on the North Shore of Oahu in Hawaii, but he's building much more at the same time.

Your turn again. What are you really good at? Think about your gifts, talents, and strengths. How can you tell? Start here: What do other people say you're good at? What do people compliment you for?

Your answers may be related to things you love, but maybe not. Your answers might seem useless in the grand scheme of life, like my friend who was always really good at loading the dishwasher. But that doesn't matter now. List whatever you're good at anyway and don't worry about trying to figure out if your answers are good enough or spiritual enough or important enough.

The Bible tells us there are different kinds of gifts, service, and work, but it's the same God working in and through them all. Check it out in 1 Corinthians 12:4–6. And that Bible passage leads us to another important lesson about gifts: they're not all about you. God doesn't give you a gift just for your own selfish use. He wants you to use your gift to touch other people's lives and help them see that God is good. The apostle Paul, writer of First Corinthians, says God intends for all those who trust in Him to fit together like a body with hands, feet, eyes, and ears. Our different gifts make us different parts of the whole. Some can sing, others can speak to big crowds, and still others are technology whizzes. And we all need each other to make God's family work.

He wants you to use your gift to touch other people's lives and help them see that God is good.

Think of your gifts as long-term loans. Have you ever heard the word *stewardship*? It means you've been given something to take care of. It's yours but not completely. In reality it belongs to God. You get to keep it, practice it, polish it, improve it, and use it for your whole life, but you're accountable to God. He is the real gift owner. What He wants to see is that you serve others and share His love through whatever gifts He's given you.

So looking at how you fit with your friends and family can help reveal gifts too. Try it. Are you a leader? Are you the one people open up to because you're a good and compassionate listener? Do you lead the team in assists? Is it easy for you to organize the group? All gifts. Write them down.

CONNECT THE DOTS

Now it's time to connect the dots. It's time to look for the connections between the backdrop of your life, your passions, and your gifts and talents. Where do they all intersect? Where in your setting can you do what you love to help other people? What direction do you need to heed to bring it all together? How can your talents point toward God? Do you hear God calling?

This isn't a kindergarten dot-to-dot. You aren't going to draw lines and come up with a finished picture of a cute doggy with a bone. It's not a magic formula that tells you what to do with your life. But it will allow you to look purposefully at how the different aspects of your life fit together. It can open your eyes to the identity God has given you and the plans He's working out for you.

If you see a match that looks interesting, pray about how you might pursue it. Ask for advice from people who know you well, including your parents, teachers, and youth leaders. And take one step in that direction. This whole process can be exciting, but maybe a little scary too. Just remember these two facts:

1. You don't have to figure out your whole life at once. You can't.

2. You're not in it alone. God promises, *"Fear not, for I have redeemed you; I have summoned you by name; you are mine"* (Isaiah 43:1).

God's not trying to hide His life plans from you. He wants to guide you one step at a time. Remember, He cares about your process of growing and learning to depend on Him.

Besides, God knows that giving us the whole thing at once would overwhelm us. Have you ever stopped and looked back to what you were doing a few months or years ago and felt surprised to be where you are now? If that hasn't happened, it will as you grow older. God's plan really is too wonderful for us to take in all at once. Showing us the whole plan would raise more questions than it answered. God is wise. He sees to it that His plan comes to us in small, digestible bites. That's how He protects us.

A wise pastor named Oswald Chambers who lived in the early 1900s said it really well in his famous book *My Utmost for His Highest*: "The call of God is like the call of the sea, no one hears it but the one who has the nature of the sea in him. It cannot be stated definitely what the call of God is to, because His call is to be in comradeship with Himself for His own purposes, and the test is to believe that God knows what He is after."

Oswald was pretty deep. Here's what he was saying: You belong to God. His nature is in you, and it's tuned to His voice and His ways like invisible wireless signals. God is calling and leading you. To what? Mostly to Himself—to trust Him and love Him and serve Him no matter what else you do. He is calling soul surfers deeper and deeper into the waters of His love and grace. Tuning your passions and gifts to His frequency will make you come alive and help you find opportunities to live out your love for God in this world.

DON'T GET DETOURED

When our friend Zach Hunter was twelve years old, he found out that slavery still existed—today, here and now, for twenty-seven million people. Not just in far-off countries, but even in his own nation, the United States. That lit a fire in Zach. He quickly became passionate about ending the injustice of slavery.

But what could a kid in Virginia do about a huge, international human-trafficking industry? He started a campaign called Loose Change to Loosen Chains (LC2LC). It was pretty simple. He asked people to donate their extra change. And he raised $8,500!

LC2LC grew, and Zach suddenly found himself in the spotlight—not a place where he was naturally comfortable. He was scared to death of public speaking. But his passion drove him on. He wanted to end slavery. If speaking to others would help, then he would do his best. Zach trusted God to provide what he needed to speak for those who didn't have a voice.

He is calling soul surfers deeper and deeper into the waters of His love and grace.

Zach kept pursuing his passion and allowed God to sharpen the skills he needed. Since then, Zach has continued to share his passion with others by speaking to millions, publishing books, and raising money to set others free.

And as God has led him on the journey, Zach has discovered another passion—encouraging teens and kids to find the gifts God has given them and to use those gifts for His purpose. If you sat down to talk with Zach, you'd find out that he'd love to have your help in his quest to end slavery. But more than that, he wants *you* to figure out what God has put in *your* heart that you can use to change the world. "Use whatever gifts God has given you for the good of others; that's why they were given to you," Zach wrote in his book *Be the Change*. "When we catch a vision for how God wants to use us and our gifts, the excitement, energy, and enjoyment that comes to us is the very definition of passion. And passion applied to a cause can change the world."

That's soul surfing! And it shows a final, important point. God will use the backdrop of your life, your passions, and your talents to reveal His calling in your life, but God is not limited by them. He's not limited by your understanding of them. He is way, way bigger than that!

He used Zach's passion to get him moving in the right direction. When Zach had bigger opportunities that required gifts he didn't even know he had, God provided His strength and helped Zach grow. That's the process He uses to lead us step-by-step.

The Bible is full of people who were called by God to do things they were *not* good at or remotely excited about. Moses tried to get out of talking to Pharaoh because he didn't speak well. Sarah laughed at the idea of having a child because she thought she was too old to bear a son. Jesus' disciples left what they had always known, fishing, to follow Him. For all of these people, God provided everything needed to follow Him and do what He called them to do.

KEEP PADDLING

In the same way, God has the power to make things happen in *your* life. He isn't limited by how things seem to be. Your job is to stay faithful, keep listening, and keep using what you've been given. Your job as a soul surfer is to stay in the water and keep paddling.

The ocean might look flat with no waves, but keep watching the horizon. God is stirring the swell. Keep living every day with your eyes and heart open. Stay in touch with God by reading the Bible, which is His letter to you, and talking to Him about what you are feeling. His waves are all around you in the small interactions of your everyday life. But the big one may be on its way.

Use the intersection of your setting, passion, and gifts to get you moving in the right direction. From there, God *"is able to do immeasurably more than all we ask or imagine, according to his power that is at work within us"* (Ephesians 3:20). That sounds like a topic for another chapter, doesn't it?

YOUR RIDE

Write down the information about your life—whatever fits and whatever comes to mind. Draw pictures too if you want.

My Setting (Including My Supporting Cast)

My Passions

My Gifts (What I'm Good At)

Got your lists? Now jot beside each item one way you can use it for God. Draw lines between the sections to connect items that fit together.

"Calling, in its fullest, is an idea too good to be true, unless and until Jesus is involved in the conversation."
—John C. Maxwell, author

"Instead of, 'You are what you do,' calling says: 'Do what you are.'"
—Os Guinness, author

"When love and skill work together, expect a masterpiece."
—John Ruskin, art critic, poet, and artist

"We are each gifted in a unique and important way. It is our privilege and our adventure to discover our own special light."
—Mary Dunbar, artist

PART 2

Forward Motion

CATCHING GOD'S WAVE

Psalm 37:4

Delight yourself in the LORD, and he will give you the desires of your heart.

Matthew 6:33

Seek first his kingdom and his righteousness, and all these things will be given to you as well.

Matthew 6:19–21

"Do not store up for yourselves treasures on earth, where moth and rust destroy, and where thieves break in and steal. But store up for yourselves treasures in heaven, where moth and rust do not destroy, and where thieves do not break in and steal. For where your treasure is, there your heart will be also."

1 Samuel 16:7

"The LORD does not look at the things man looks at. Man looks at the outward appearance, but the LORD looks at the heart."

Ephesians 3.20

To him who is able to do immeasurably more than all we ask or imagine, according to his power that is at work within us.

1 Corinthians 9:25

Everyone who competes in the games goes into strict training. They do it to get a crown that will not last; but we do it to get a crown that will last forever.

CHAPTER 4

DREAM ON

"From the moment I caught my first wave, I knew that I wanted to be a pro surfer. Nothing else seemed to matter."

—*Bethany Hamilton in the movie* SOUL SURFER

In the movie SOUL SURFER, *when Bethany wins a local surfing competition, legendary surfer Ben Aipa tells Bethany's parents, "You're doing a great job training her brother Tom. Looks like Bethany could have a real future as a pro." Ben later adds, "With her will and her heart, she'll go far." Bethany Hamilton was, and is, a dreamer. She has salt water running through her veins, and she didn't just want to surf as a part-time hobby. No way. She had much bigger plans than that. Bethany wanted to be a pro—one of the people who surf for a living. She wanted to push her abilities to the limit and compete against the top surfers in the world.*

Bethany dreams big, but she's not the only one. You're about to meet another teenage dreamer.

He trudged on step-by-step, higher and higher. Finally, there was no farther or higher to go. Jordan Romero stood on top of the world, for real. He had reached the summit of Mount Everest, the tallest peak in the world at 29,035 feet. What did he do on top? He called his mom on a satellite phone. Jordan was thirteen on May 22, 2010, when he became the youngest person ever to climb the massive mountain.

Everest is a dangerous place. Climbers die there; it's not uncommon. Some fall off cliffs. Some get lost and freeze when killer storms blow in. Many get swelling and fluid in their brains or lungs from being in the Death Zone. Once humans get higher than twenty-six-thousand feet, our bodies start starving for oxygen; there's just not enough in that thin air. Sounds inviting, doesn't it? Most climbers who go that high breathe from oxygen bottles, but the effects can still take a deadly toll on their bodies.

That's why many people argued that Jordan shouldn't have been on Everest at all. Too young. Too much could have gone wrong.

Maybe. But Jordan had a dream. "Every step I take is finally toward the biggest goal of my life, to stand on top of the world," he wrote on his blog before the expedition. He didn't take his quest lightly. He seriously trained for it with his dad and step mom. He climbed small mountains and other big mountains that were still smaller than Everest. (Another one of his goals was to climb the Seven Summits, the highest peak on each of the world's continents. After Everest, he had only one of those left.) And Jordan speaks to classes and kids' groups to encourage them to get outside and pursue their passions. The way he puts it is, "Find your Everest."

Jordan had a big dream, and he committed everything he had to reach it.

IMAGINE ALL THE DREAMERS

What would the world be like without dreamers? It would certainly be a very different and much less interesting place.

Martin Luther King Jr. had a dream. It was a famous dream of equality and justice for all people, regardless of the color of their skin. It looked like an impossible dream at the time, and it cost him his life. But it's a dream his children and grandchildren saw come true and a dream that continues to become more and more real with every passing day.

Walt Disney had a dream that animation, film, characters, stories, and amusement parks could bring inspiration and refreshment to people of all walks of life. He said, "My business is making people, especially children, happy." Look around Disney World or Disneyland, and you will see that his dream is alive and well.

Vivaldi, Bach, Handel, and many other great composers and musicians through time dreamed up inspiring, heart-moving music that would impact the souls of listeners. The world still listens to their creations today.

Louis Pasteur had a dream that people could live longer, healthier lives if disease and infection could be limited through scientific advancements. The vaccines that resulted from his work have saved the lives of millions.

Leonardo da Vinci dreamed of flying. The great artist and inventor sketched and designed potential flying machines way back about five hundred years ago. He never saw his dream of flight realized, but it still inspires us today.

Those dreamers are only the beginning. Think of any activity or field, and you can probably think of somebody who dreams of taking it farther than ever before. Go ahead and try. Who else can you think of who has changed the world or your life by pursuing their dreams?

1.
_____

2.
_____

3.
_____

YOUR DREAMS

Dreams bring focus to your passions and gifts. As the dots connect, and you listen for God's voice softly speaking to you, you get a glimpse of what you want to do with it all. It's a target you can take aim at. It's a goal you can work toward. It's the soul surfer's wave on the horizon, and it's time to start paddling. It's time to go for God's adventure!

So ... do you know what your dream might be? Is something taking shape in your heart and mind? Is it playing varsity ball? Becoming a journalist? Getting into a good college? The list could go on and on. What has God put in your heart?

It is a good thing dreams are born from our passions, because it takes a lot of passion to keep pursuing a dream. Dreams are exciting, adventurous, and fun, but they also take sacrifice. Nobody reaches a dream in one step. Jordan Romero didn't start on Mount Everest. Peyton Manning didn't immediately play in the Super Bowl. And U2 didn't leap straight into stadium tours. Anyone who has ever achieved a dream has had to work, practice, sweat, and fight through challenges and obstacles. They've had to make an inconvenient choice—who wants to practice scales when everybody's going out for mongo-frappa-spress-iattas?

But having a dream keeps you moving in the right direction, even when you're not totally sure how you're going to get there. And it guides the choices you make along the way like a lighthouse keeps you on track even in the fog.

DIFFERENT KINDS OF DREAMS

Before we go any further, let's make sure we're all on the same page with this dream stuff. When we talk about dreams, it can get confusing because our English language has one word for at least three different kinds of dreams.

Sleep dreams are the ones you have when you're asleep. There's a lot scientists don't know about why we have dreams or where exactly they come from, but basically they're subconscious thoughts that are rambling around in your brain while you sleep.

Sometimes, God steps in, organizes those rambling thoughts, and gives them a special meaning for a special purpose. The Bible talks about people like Joseph, who had dreams that were messages from God about their lives, and like Daniel, who had the gift from God of interpreting other people's special dreams. But most of the time, our sleep dreams are just a way for our brains to kick back and take some time off.

How many times have you awakened and said, "I had the craziest dream last night"? Sometimes, you

But having a dream keeps you moving in the right direction, even when you're not totally sure how you're going to get there.

can find a connection to life—maybe you've been struggling to finish a class paper and you have a dream that you're climbing a mountain but can never get to the top. Or you watch a scary movie and wake up in the sweat of a nightmare. But most of the time, the images and ideas that stream through your sleep dreams aren't significant.

These dreams are a natural part of our lives, but they're not what we mean when we talk about pursuing our dreams. Then again, it *would* be really cool to fly like we do in dreams, wouldn't it?

Fantasy dreams are idealized ideas of stuff we like or that sounds appealing. Kids often dream of being superheroes and beautiful princesses. They dream of galaxies or castles far away. They dream of lands full of candy trees and rivers of chocolate milk where they can swim and drink at the same time. Maybe you still daydream about that yourself. But kids don't really want to move to a faraway kingdom or wear a red spandex suit and a cape for the rest of their lives. Fantasies represent imaginations and what-ifs. They can be natural and fun, a way to exercise your imagination, but not something to base a lifetime on.

Life dreams are what we're talking about. These are the realistic, inspired goals people have for their lives. They are based in reality, yet inspired by a desire to go beyond what *is* to what can *be*. These dreams are desires to do, experience, or become extraordinary. They might be inspired by what you've seen others do or by a thought or idea God has placed inside you. Either way, life dreams are accomplished by taking everyday steps toward what you want to happen someday.

Big dreams look different for different people.

Life dreams can actually be accomplished apart from God. There are plenty of people who don't believe in God who achieve their dreams. Their dreams even resonate with the gifts God gave them, even though they don't recognize God in those dreams. God places no demands on the talents and dreams He puts in people's lives. They are ours to keep with no strings attached. But how much better it is to travel toward your dreams with your hand in God's hand. You can be sure you will miss out on nothing, and you will always have someone to share your joy, your frustration, your excitement, your impatience, and all your emotions with.

OLYMPIC DREAMS

The Olympics are a dream theater. They're the ultimate arena for watching the triumph of human dreams come true and the heartbreak of those that don't.

Most Olympic athletes start young, with passion and talent that grows into a dream to be the best in the world—sometimes at some pretty weird sports. That's what makes the Olympic Games so awesome. Most of the athletes aren't professionals. They still have to work real jobs like the rest of us because there's no pro badminton, handball, or luge league. (You should read about some of the exhibition sports through the years, like skijoring. It's skiing behind a horse. Awesome!) No matter how unknown the sport, its athletes have made serious sacrifices in time and money. They've trained years for one shot at a medal. Their desire and vision drives them toward achieving their dreams.

Bryan Clay is one of those athletes. He might actually be the greatest athlete in the world, and it's possible you've never heard of him. Bryan is a *decathlete,* which means he competes in the decathlon. Talk about tough! It's really ten sports in one. Decathletes have to be good at the 100-meter sprint, long jump, shot put, high jump, 400-meter run, 110-meter high hurdles, discus, pole vault, javelin, and 1500-meter run. Whew! It takes some serious effort just to read them all.

Bryan's dream was winning an Olympic gold medal in the decathlon. It's the pinnacle of decathlon competition, and Bryan had been competing since his teen years. That's when the decathlon became an escape for him. Bryan's childhood had been hard due to messy family problems, and he had gotten in trouble with drinking and drugs during his teens. Competing gave him a healthy way out and a pathway to college. And college was where he met Jesus and turned over his life to Him. After that, Bryan's dream had an eternal component. It was about more than his own fame or glory; it was about showing people what God's presence meant in his life and touching other people's lives however he could.

Bryan won the silver medal at the 2004 Athens Olympics and then worked his way back to the 2008 Games in Beijing, China. There, he won the gold. It was a dream come true. But even more important to Bryan was being used to show others how good and glorious God is. That's why he started a foundation to help troubled kids overcome struggles like he once faced.

BIG DREAMS

As you begin to wake up your dreams, dream big!

God wants you to look beyond the limitations around you and trust Him to open up the possibilities before you. Why? Because He's huge. He's powerful and mighty. He's created things we can't even comprehend, things that baffle even our nerdiest scientists. A man named Job, in the Bible, talks about some amazing things God does, but then he reminds us that even those things are only the tip of the iceberg concerning who He is. *"And these are but the outer fringe of his works; how faint the whisper we hear of him! Who then can understand the thunder of his power?"* (Job 26:14). Yet in all His awesome power, God loves and cares for His people, giving them power and strength (Psalm 68:35). And Ephesians 3:20 tells us He's able to do things within us that we can't even imagine! And He's able to do that for each of us.

Big dreams look different for different people. An athlete may dream of winning a championship, while someone suffering from disease or injury may dream of walking across the room. One person can dream of sailing around the world, while someone else dreams of having the chance to go to school. Dreams are personal—just like God is personal. He does a unique work in each of our hearts. God has a specific dream for each person. He has a specific dream for you. No matter how young or old you are, or what your present circumstances might be, you can achieve the dream God has put in your heart.

Josiah Viera had a ginormous dream and faith that he could reach it. Nobody else was too sure of that. They knew that Josiah was a walking miracle already. He'd been on the verge of death for most of his life, and at six years old, he was barely taller than two feet and weighed only fifteen pounds. Think about that. Some babies are born weighing ten pounds! Most six-year-olds weigh more in the fifty-pound range. Josiah is so small because he has an incredibly rare disease called Hutchinson-Gilford progeria syndrome or premature-aging syndrome. Basically, Josiah's body wears out and breaks down about ten times faster than it should. His organs and body systems have the problems of a sixty-year-old instead of a six-year-old.

Despite all that, Josiah dreamed of playing baseball on a team. He was crazy about the game. It's all he wanted to do. He could barely hold a bat, but he could hit the ball. Finally, Josiah got his chance. A local T-ball team heard about Josiah and invited him to come play a game with them. The little baseball lover was all over it! And he didn't even need the tee. He told the coach to pitch him the ball. He hit it every time and ran the bases glowing with joy. His dream came true. He didn't want it to end.

A few weeks later, it got even better. After Josiah got out of the hospital (again), the team invited him to join them for the rest of the season. Josiah returned to the diamond. And for the final game, about one thousand people came out to cheer him on. Josiah's mom carried him around the ballpark afterward, and he high-fived everyone in sight.

You have access to the God of the universe, the creator and giver of dreams.

Josiah's name comes from the Bible and means "God has healed." Josiah's life on earth was expected to be short. When ESPN asked him what he thought heaven might look like, Josiah answered, "Jesus." No matter how Josiah does end up living, he has no doubt that God can help him achieve his dreams. He already has. Josiah's mom says her son had been put on earth to touch people's lives. He has certainly achieved that dream, as well.

Across the ocean, Pascal and Leno Mwanchoka were dreaming their own big dreams. Theirs might sound strange to you if you often sit in class daydreaming about being anywhere besides school. Kids in Africa are dreaming of being right where you are. Millions of them live in slums where the opportunity for an education is almost impossible. Actually, for many of them that dream is a dream beyond a dream. They're simply dreaming of getting enough food to eat each day.

That was the case for Pascal and his brother Leno. Their mother was an alcoholic. At thirteen, Pascal was living on the streets of Nairobi, Kenya, scavenging scrap metal to try to get money to buy food for him and his younger brother. They often went to sleep without eating. So when the brothers were invited to attend a free school, where shoes were optional and they would get a free meal each day, the boys said yes. Their big dream went from simply surviving another day to reaching a better life through education—maybe a life beyond poverty. Pascal and Leno still lived in a shelter and collected scrap metal, but they were given the gift of expanding their dreams.

You have the opportunity to dream. You have the resources to start toward your dream. You probably already have a dream in your heart, or at least the

seed of a dream. You have access to the God of the universe, the creator and giver of dreams. You have His promises to help you all along the way. Be the dreamer He has made you to be. Dream big! Aim high! And get going!

YOUR RIDE

Give yourself something to shoot for. Make a list of the things you'd like to do in your life. Anything. Everything. Don't worry about how you're going to make it happen. Just dream big. Talk to God about your list and add to it regularly. Here are some categories to get you started.

This year, I want to . . .

_____

_____

While I'm in high school, I want to . . .

_____

_____

If I have a family, I want to . . .

_____

_____

I want to ... in my life.

_____

_____

Bonus Challenge: Go back and write one step you can take for each goal or dream you wrote down.

"A dream is the bearer of a new possibility, the enlarged horizon, the great hope."
—Howard Thurman, American theologian

"Go confidently in the direction of your dreams. Live the life you have imagined."
—Henry David Thoreau, author

"Hold fast to dreams, for if dreams die, life is a broken-winged bird that cannot fly."
—Langston Hughes, American poet

"All our dreams can come true, if we have the courage to pursue them."
—Walt Disney, Filmmaker

"Catch on fire with enthusiasm and people will come for miles to watch you burn."
—John Wesley, Christian theologian

CHAPTER 5

YOUR PLACE IN THE LINEUP

"It looks like I'm not going to be able to go to Mexico, so I brought some things for the orphanage."

–Bethany Hamilton to her youth leader, Sarah Hill

In the movie SOUL SURFER, *there is a scene in which Bethany decides to skip going on a mission trip with her youth group in order to stay home and train for a big surf contest. When Sarah, her youth leader questions her decision, Bethany wrestles with her dreams and priorities and how they fit together.*

You'll have times like Bethany too, as you try to choose and follow God's priorities. You'll wonder if going His way will move you toward fulfilling your dreams or take you farther away from them. And you'll wonder if you can really trust Him. In this chapter, we'll talk about how your dreams fit with God's bigger plan.

Kelly Clark had a dream, a few of them actually. They all had to do with snowboarding, including winning X Games gold and an Olympic gold medal. She grew up in Vermont. And when she was a teen, she threw everything she had into being the best female snowboarder in the world. She trained and practiced and organized her life around snowboarding. Nobody could come close to Kelly's skills in the half pipe. And you know what? Kelly achieved all her life's dreams by the time she was eighteen, including winning gold medals at the X Games and Olympics.

She did it. She reached the top, and it was fun—for a little while. Then, the fame and money and travel all just felt ... empty. Kelly had pursued her dreams apart from God, and all her success and rewards left her unfulfilled. She was sick of life. What she'd always wanted wasn't what she thought it would be.

That's when Kelly started hearing about Jesus. She found out God loved her. She discovered there was more, much more, than her big-time snowboarding life. She gave her life to God. He readjusted her priorities and brought her a peace and fulfillment she'd never known existed. She even put a big sticker on the nose of her snowboard that says, "Jesus, I cannot hide my love" because she can't. Kelly loves Jesus so much she wants Him to be first in everything in her life, even her life's passion, snowboarding.

Kelly kept winning X Games. She returned to two more Olympics and claimed another bronze medal. She continues to accomplish her big dreams and enjoy what's even better than gold: God's peace, fulfillment, and love.

Kelly found out how God turns our life priorities upside down—not in a bad way—in an awesome way! When she put God first in everything, she discovered that He gave her all she needed and much more on the inside. She discovered that when we commit ourselves to Him first, the rest of life falls into place.

PUTTING GOD FIRST

So that's how Kelly learned to put God first in her life. But what about you? What would that look like in your life?

When Jesus was on earth, He told His disciples, *"Seek first his kingdom and his righteousness, and all these things will be given to you as well"* (Matthew 6:33). Wow! Great promise, right?

So you may be thinking: *So all I have to do is glance God's way, maybe say a prayer each morning and go to church, and He'll give me whatever I want? He'll make my dreams come true? Awesome!*

Uh, no. Not so fast! Trusting God to achieve your dream requires an all-out commitment. It means letting your faith rule when it's easy and all your friends are cheering you on—and when it's not so easy and even a little scary.

That's what seeking God's kingdom first is all about. It's about going all in. It's not dabbing a toe in the pool; it's doing a cannonball with the biggest splash you can muster. That's the way soul surfers roll. They're not casual. They're radical. They commit their lives to God and don't look back, and they discover that living life with Him is the greatest adventure ever. It's better than anything we could ever come up with on our own. There's no wave to ride through life like God's wave.

We may be the ones who live the dream but God's the one who gives the dreams.

The problem is that we tend to think of God in human terms. We've had so many people disappoint us and lie to us that we suspect that God is like that too. Now, you would never dare say that out loud (especially to your church friends), but deep down in your heart you sometimes feel that way. You think, *What if I follow Him and I go down in flames? What if He really isn't telling me to do this? What if my way really is the best way?* Admit it. Sometimes, you actually believe that last one!

Well, that is why the Bible says we walk by faith. Sometimes, it takes faith to go out on that limb. But when you know He is leading you and you have scripture to back you up, you need to go for it! Don't let fear stand in your way! Don't miss out on the great things God has for you.

God will never lead you where He won't take care of you. He loves to give His children good gifts. He sees the big picture and wants to give you what He knows is best. So give Him your heart. He is worthy of your trust.

WHO COMES FIRST?

A *lineup* in surfing is where the surfers wait to catch the waves. There's an order to it. The more experienced and local surfers are usually closer to the spot where the best waves break and where they can catch them. Others rotate through too, but everyone has to pay attention. Is there someone already on a wave who has the right-of-way? Are they in a good spot to even catch this wave? Surfers have to know who goes first to avoid crashes and wipeouts. It makes the ride much more fun.

There's another kind of lineup in sports. It's the order a coach puts the team into to determine who's going to start the game and who will substitute when needed. In baseball and softball, it shows in what order the players will bat. Does a coach draw names out of a hat to determine a lineup? No way. He looks at the whole team, including its strengths and weaknesses, and makes decisions to give the team its best chance of winning.

God is like our coach in real life, and when we seek Him first, we let Him set up our lineup. Why? Because God has plans and purposes in mind that we can't possibly understand yet. Because we realize that He sees the bigger picture; He knows our strengths and weaknesses even better than we do. He sees everything—our past, present, and future all at once—like one of those coaches in a tower who can look down and see the whole field. But we can only see the part of the field right in front of us or the big opponent ready to squash us. God can see the open space behind. He knows how best to get us across the goal line. Sometimes, His instructions might sound weird. They might not look like they take us toward reaching our dream. We think, *You want me to what? But* ... And He reminds us, "Trust Me. Listen carefully to Me and do what I tell you. I want to get you through this and work it out for your best." God knows where we fit best in the lineup, and He helps us keep our priorities in order. He wants to give us the best chance of winning over all the challenges in our lives.

Seeking God first is remembering that He's the Coach and we're the players. He's the King, and we're the servants. He's the Master, and we're the apprentices. We may be the ones who live the dream but God's the one who gives the dreams. Putting Him first, letting Him decide your lineup, and following His ways are the best things you can ever do for yourself.

See, God isn't one of those mean coaches who shouts and spits and cusses out His players. He loves us unconditionally. He's the kind of coach who encourages and teaches us the skills we need. He wants to help us avoid unexpected dangers and costly mistakes. He knows how to use the opponents and challenges we face to make us better and stronger. We fail when we try to play with our own game plan, but when we follow His plan for us, we have access to all His strategy and grace so we can succeed. However, He leaves the choice to us.

ALL DAY EVERY DAY

Where do you begin to put God first in your life and plans? Your first choice must be to give your heart to God, if you haven't done that already. If you have, you know how it changes everything. God is as close as your breath, ready to walk with you through the process of changing how you think and live and what you see as important. He will show you how to understand His lineup and priorities, and the more you do, the easier and more natural it will become.

You should know that choosing to seek and follow God isn't a one-time thing. It's a 24-7 deal, even when it's hard. Sometimes, it will seem easy to do, like during camp, in a youth group meeting, or when there are other people around trying to do the same thing. But other times, you might feel like you're the only one trying to do it, and God's game plan looks upside down to you.

It can be confusing at times. Remember Jesus' disciples? They were the twelve guys who hung out with Him all the time, every day. They got to tell Him their doubts and ask Him their questions—and they still didn't always understand the stuff He was teaching about. If anybody should have gotten the idea of how to seek God's priorities and follow His game plans on the way to their dreams, it should have been them, right?

But guess what, it took them a while. Even though Jesus told them His priorities were about serving other people, a couple of the disciples argued about how they could get the most power for themselves. When Jesus welcomed kids and outcasts, they tried to tell those people to go away. And when Jesus told them His game plan included his death, they said, "No way! We won't let it happen!" They thought their dream was to see Jesus rule. It wasn't a wrong dream, but God had an entirely different idea from theirs of what that looked like.

The beauty of the disciples is that Jesus always loved them and helped them. There must have been times He thought, *How dense can you guys be?* But like a good coach, He helped to show them His ways. He gave them all the information they could handle and then asked them to trust Him for the rest. He helped them learn and change their perspective. Still, they were brokenhearted when Jesus died on the cross. They thought their dream had ended for good. But they were overjoyed when they saw Him resurrected. Then, they understood!

Your soul-surfing journey will have a lot in common with what Jesus' disciples went through. You won't always get things right, and you'll definitely have times when you have to decide to let God direct your dreams and priorities, even if things don't seem to be going the way you expect.

So, okay, it's time for a little quiz! Let's see what you can learn about seeking God's priorities first in your everyday life.

1. You want to get someone's attention—like, romantically. So the first thing you do is:

   a. Buy some new clothes hoping that special person will notice.

   b. Text your friends all day about how much you like your potential love interest.

   c. Pray about it and ask God to guide you in the relationship.

2. You have options for Friday night. Which will you choose?

   a. Go to the party at your friend's house—everyone will be there.

   b. Stay home and watch a movie with your dog.

   c. Help babysit for a group of single moms who need a night off.

3. Your grandparents just gave you a hundred dollars for your birthday.

   a. You whip out the wish list of stuff you didn't get for Christmas and start shopping.

   b. You take it straight to the bank to put in savings toward college.

   c. Before anything else, you give part of it to your church or a charity that cares for the poor.

4. You need a 90 percent on your math test to pass the class. Your supersmart classmate has all the answers, uncovered in plain sight. Do you:

   a. Copy away—it's your lucky day.

   b. Only glance at the ones you can't figure out. Passing this class is a key to your future.

   c. Keep your eyes on your own paper, trusting that God will direct your life no matter what happens with this class.

5. When you're feeling down or lonely, you:

a. Listen to depressing music until you cry yourself to sleep.

b. Look at pictures of old friends and remember the good times.

c. Ask God to help you think of someone else who might be lonely; then give that person a call.

Hopefully, the right answers were pretty obvious to you. Just in case, *C* was always the best option. But real life is not always so clear cut. And even when it is, it's not always easy to do things God's way and put Him first.

When you find yourself caught in that tension between what might seem like a simple solution and what God says is right, it's always smart to do things God's way. You don't know what's around the next corner, but God does.

HE IS GOOD

You might be asking yourself, *What do those everyday decisions have to do with reaching my dreams?* Well, the answer is everything. Choosing God's priorities will help you stay pointed in His direction. It will help His priorities become part of your heart and mind, and it will help shape you and focus your dreams on what God wants them to be. It will also teach you how to listen to God's guidance when it's hard to know which direction will take you where you need to go.

The movie *Soul Surfer* shows Bethany Hamilton wrestling with her dreams and priorities and how they fit together. She ran into some uncertainty when faced with the decision of whether to stay home and train for a big surf contest or go on a mission trip with her youth group. She told her mother she felt torn and didn't know what to do. (Talking to your mom is always a good choice when you feel confused.) Bethany's mom saw a bigger picture. She called wrestling with the decision "a small step in a good direction." What kind of an answer was that? Did Bethany's mom want her to suffer? Not at all. But she saw the situation like "Coach God." She knew seeking God and trusting Him with confusing decisions would help Bethany get to know and understand God better. And Bethany's mom knew God was big enough to guide Bethany and help her get back on track if she made the wrong call.

You'll have times like Bethany too, as you try to choose and follow God's priorities. You'll wonder if going His way will move you toward fulfilling your dreams or take you farther away from them. And you'll wonder if you can really trust Him.

When it comes down to it, there's no way to figure out ahead of time exactly what you'll get out of putting God first. But that's the wrong way to look at it anyway. You can't see tomorrow no matter whose ways you're following. But you do know you can trust in God's goodness, His love, and His promises to carry you no matter where your journey leads.

Have you seen the movie *The Lion, the Witch, and the Wardrobe* or read the book? The main characters—Peter, Susan, Edmund, and Lucy—are hearing for the first time about someone named Aslan in the land of Narnia. It's a magical land, and they're talking to a pair of beavers about Aslan. The beavers tell them this Aslan isn't a person, he's a lion. And he's the true king of Narnia. *What? A lion? Lions eat people!* The kids ask if this lion king is safe. And one of the beavers answers, "Safe? ... 'Course he isn't safe, but he's good. He's the King, I tell you."

Jesus is the same way. He's not tame. He doesn't do whatever we tell Him to do. He takes us on adventures that might feel scary at times, and He can blow our minds with His incredible strength. But He's amazingly good and loving and trustworthy. He's able to turn the worst in our lives into the best. He sees a whole eternal picture that we only get glimpses of and in that ultimate eternity, we're guaranteed goodness beyond imagination. Try trusting Him so much that you put Him first in everything you do. It's the way of the soul surfer. Soul surfers keep riding the wave even when life isn't looking exactly like they want it. They keep putting God first and letting Him reorder what's most important. And they experience His awesome love and goodness all along the way.

> *He sees a whole eternal picture that we only get glimpses of—and in that ultimate eternity, we're guaranteed goodness beyond imagination.*

YOUR RIDE

Take a jar and fill it with the largest seashells that will fit inside. (You can use rocks if you don't have any shells.) Then fill in all around the shells with sand. Now, dump it all out into a container and start over. Try putting the sand in the jar first, followed by the shells. They won't fit.

Our lives are the same—when we mix up our priorities and fill our lives with all kinds of little things before God's big priorities, it doesn't all fit. The only way it works is to put God first.

List some God things you need to prioritize in your life:

_____

_____

_____

_____

_____

List some little things that feel big so you often end up filling your life with them first:

_____

_____

_____

_____

_____

_____

"You can't get second things by putting them first; you can get second things only by putting first things first."

—C.S. Lewis, author

"Put God first in anything and everything that you think, say and do."

—Randy Pausch, professor

CHAPTER 6

X MARKS THE SPOT

"Every day between now and regionals, when I'm in the water training, I'll be thinking about you, Hamilton."

–Malina Birch to Bethany Hamilton in the movie SOUL SURFER

In the movie SOUL SURFER, *we get to see Bethany compete in several surfing competitions. At the end of a big tournament, like a regional or national championship, the winner gets to hoist a ginormous trophy. To many surfers, that trophy is exactly the kind of treasure they're looking for. Think about Bethany's surfing rival, Malina Birch. Malina is so focused on winning (and beating Bethany) that she will do almost anything to keep Bethany from catching a good wave.*

What about you? What do you view as treasure, and do you think God has a different perspective? Read on, and you'll get to dig into the idea of real treasure.

~~~

"Argh, matey!" The jolly roger flew ragged above the ship's dark hull. Its skull and crossbones flapped in the breeze as the pirates watched anxiously for land. They studied their map. "The treasure should be just beyond that cove. Soon it will be ours!"

The scurvy knaves laughed menacingly and rounded the point into the cove. They lowered their anchor and rowed for shore in the longboat. The map showed an *X* in the valley beyond the mountain ridge to the south. It would be too hard a hike for Patchwork Pete and his peg leg, so he stayed to guard the longboat. The others set off for the treasure.

Hours later, they began digging in the sandy soil, hopeful that this was indeed the right spot. When they unearthed the skull, they knew the treasure couldn't be far below. Sure enough, a shovel soon struck something solid. Now they dug with renewed speed and pulled up the heavy box filled with gold bricks and coins. The treasure was theirs!

It was hard work dragging the treasure chest back over the mountain and down to the shore. Their arms ached as they rowed the longboat back to the ship. Captain Crunchy the Kidd was pleased. He ordered the anchor to be raised and the sails to be unfurled.

That's when the *Scourge of the Deep*, the ship of the rival pirate Captain Shebeard, rounded the point. The crew knew Shebeard wasn't coming in peace. Captain Crunchy tried to sail for open seas, but the ship's escape route was blocked. Cannons boomed, and pirates snarled. The ships pulled side to side, and the marauders swung onto the enemy decks. When the smoke cleared, Captain Shebeard had stolen the treasure and left Captain Crunchy's crew walking the plank.

Just another day in the thieving lives of treasure-hungry pirates.

TREASURE CHEST

What? You don't think that tale could make it into *Pirates of the Caribbean*? Okay, but we had to talk about pirates if we're going to talk about treasure. And treasure is our main point here.

What is a treasure? It could be ...

- a box full of gold.
- a bank account full of money.
- jewelry, art, or other valuable collectibles.
- something you're attached to because of its meaning.
- something given to you by someone you care about.
- your health.
- your family.

A treasure is anything really valuable—and that can be different for different people.

- your friends.
- your car.
- your home.
- your freedom.

A treasure is anything really valuable—and that can be different for different people. No matter what the treasure, people are willing to make great sacrifices in order to get it and keep it.

Pirates risk their lives to pursue hidden treasure. Some guys sacrifice their integrity and purity in order to gain popularity and acceptance. Some girls risk their health and self-respect trying to gain the perfect body.

But some sacrifices are positive. Athletes sacrifice their time and energy in order to compete at higher levels. Good students sacrifice free time and maybe some sleep in order to feed their minds and achieve higher levels of learning. Parents make sacrifices all the time for the children they cherish.

TRUE TREASURE HUNTERS

The problem with the pirate approach to treasure is exactly what our friends in the opening story above found out. You can work really hard to secure your treasure, but it doesn't last. Have you ever seen the bumper sticker that says, "He who dies with the most toys wins"? That would have been a good one for the ancient Egyptians to slap on the rumps of their camels. They thought they would need all their valuables in the afterlife, so they packed them into big, fancy pyramid-shaped graves. Are they living it up with all their gold and jewelry and boats and clothes now? Nope, we're still digging up their buried treasures in pyramids today.

When we die, the toys get left behind. And if our only treasure is our toys, then all our treasure is gone too. But there is another way—a better way. It's about digging into our lives for a treasure of *giving* instead of a treasure of getting.

Mother Teresa is famous for giving up every kind of earthly treasure. She went to live among the poorest of the poor in Calcutta, India, for forty-five years. She helped orphans, HIV/AIDS victims, and people who were starving. She received lots of recognition and awards during her lifetime, but it was a hard way to live. Even she got discouraged, but Mother Teresa's great reward was waiting for her in heaven. If you can be rich in heaven, she's loaded.

On the other end of the spectrum, picture one billion dollars. What does that even look like? How do you measure it? Try this: do you know how many Chipotle burritos you could buy with a billion dollars? 142,857,142. You could also buy plenty of cars, computers, houses, boats, and tropical islands with a billion dollars.

It's about digging into our lives for a treasure of giving instead of a treasure of getting.

So imagine what a multibillionaire could buy. And imagine how a billionaire could change the world by giving that money away. That's exactly what one group of billionaires is doing. The Giving Pledge was started by the two richest men in the United States, investor Warren Buffett and Microsoft founder Bill Gates. Those guys realized that money isn't everything. They challenged billionaires to make a pledge to give 50 percent or more of their fortunes to charity, either during their lifetimes or after they die. And Buffett and Gates led by example.

Do those billionaires know God? We don't know. But their decision is more about giving than getting. By giving away some of their fortunes, they are showing others the way to avoid hoarding their wealth, which they'll lose anyway when they die. That's a wonderful thing in this life.

But when we give our hearts to God, something even more amazing happens. The earthly treasure we give away, whatever it may be, is replaced by a treasure that really lasts. As we give away our time, money, knowledge, and skills to serve others, we find true treasure—love, forgiveness, humility, service, compassion—building in our lives. Really, it's about creating more of the kind of stuff we give and share instead of the kind we get and guard. That's God's kind of soul surfing treasure. It fills us up with much deeper joy and satisfaction, and it lasts forever. It keeps paying off.

Who do you know whose treasure is more heavenly than earthly? They don't have to be billionaires or live in poverty. They can be students at your school who put other people first through smiles and kindness. They might be members of your family who choose to do the right thing over the convenient thing. Or they could be heroes in your community who sacrifice their time and talents to help and care for others. They could be somebody like Mackenzie.

Thirteen-year-old Mackenzie Bearup could have been doing just about anything other girls her age like to do: playing a sport, taking music lessons, or hanging out with her friends. Instead, she started collecting books and donating them to abused and homeless children around the country. After only three years, by January 2011, she had given away more than fifty-seven thousand books.

Mackenzie discovered that reading helps ease the severe pain she feels from a disease called reflex sympathetic dystrophy. Getting into a book takes her mind off of her own suffering, and she wanted to share that same relief with others. She started by filling up a library at a new children's hospital with three hundred books. Then she kept going. Mackenzie asks other people to donate the books, and she and her family collect them and deliver them to the shelters. Her efforts bring hope and enjoyment to kids who need them.

YOUR RIDE

Want some ideas for storing up treasure in heaven instead of on earth? Choose one of these or think of your own to do this week:

- Volunteer to help serve a meal at a local homeless shelter.

- Spend time praying for a friend who is going through a difficult time.

- Go through your closet and donate some of your clothes to a charity.

- Write a praise poem to God.

- Set aside some specific time to talk with a friend who is struggling or hurting.

- Sponsor a child through an organization like Compassion International or World Vision.

- Take homemade cookies to your elderly neighbor.

"Never forget what Jesus did for you. Never take lightly what it cost Him. And never assume that if it cost Him his very life, that it won't also cost you yours."

—Rich Mullins, Christian musician

"He is no fool who gives what he cannot keep to gain that which he cannot lose."

—Jim Elliott, missionary

"My mother always said that every time you do a good deed here on earth, you're storing up a treasure in heaven."

—Robert G. Lee, minister

"He who lays up treasures in heaven looks forward to eternity; he's moving daily toward his treasures."

—Randy Alcorn, author of The Treasure Principle

PART 3

In the Impact Zone

CATCHING GOD'S WAVE

Jeremiah 29:11

"I know the plans I have for you," declares the LORD, "plans to prosper you and not to harm you, plans to give you hope and a future."

1 Corinthians 2:9 NLT

"No eye has seen, no ear has heard, and no mind has imagined what God has prepared for those who love him."

2 Corinthians 4:17

Our light and momentary troubles are achieving for us an eternal glory that far outweighs them all.

John 16:33

[Jesus answered], "In this world you will have trouble. But take heart! I have overcome the world."

Psalm 138:7

Though I walk in the midst of trouble, you preserve my life; you stretch out your hand against the anger of my foes, with your right hand you save me.

Psalm 32:7 NCV

You are my hiding place. You protect me from my troubles and fill me with songs of salvation.

CHAPTER 7

WHEN BAD THINGS HAPPEN

"Life is an adventure, and sometimes you wipe out and end up in the impact zone."

–Bethany Hamilton in the movie SOUL SURFER

In the movie SOUL SURFER, there's a scene in which Bethany is surfing in her first competition since the shark attack, and she winds up being totally pounded by some really big waves. Surfers call that area the impact zone. It's a pretty descriptive name, don't you think? That's the place where the waves break the hardest, and if a surfer gets stuck there, the crashing waves slam down on them and flip them around like they're in a big washing machine.

Why do we all sometimes end up in the impact zone, and where's God in all of that tumbling, crashing, and pounding? In this chapter we're going to talk about hanging onto God when you land in the impact zone of life.

Did you know you can get insurance against alien abduction? We kid you not. Buy the insurance, and if you're ever beamed into space by alien invaders, the insurance company GRIP (that's short for Goodfellow Rebecca Ingrams Pearson, which sounds much more boring) will pay you $1.5 million. The same company will also insure you against turning into a werewolf, getting injured by a ghost, and being smashed by an asteroid.

Those are some of the weirdest insurance policies, but there's no shortage of stuff you can pay an insurance company to "protect" you from—by *protect*, they mean pay for the damages if and when it happens. You can insure your pets, your voice (Bruce Springsteen has), your rare-bottle-cap collection, your smile, and just about any other body part or possession you want to. Once you get old enough to drive a car, you'll discover you're required by law to insure your car. Then they pay to fix your car or the other car if you crash. (If your parents are supergenerous, they might cover the cost of insurance for you. Better start saving now, though, just in case.)

People pay huge amounts of money to protect themselves in case bad things happen. The funny thing is they make all the names sound nice and happy even though the insurance usually works when the bad stuff hits. Check it out: Health insurance is for when you get sick. Life insurance pays if you die. Home insurance takes care of when your house burns down, blows up, or gets hit by a meteor—oops, no, they call meteors "acts of God" and won't pay for those unless you buy a separate insurance policy just for that. Oh, and you also must have separate flood insurance if you want to fix your house after it goes underwater.

Is your head spinning yet? If you're looking for a future career with lots of job security, you might want to look into selling insurance. It's not going away anytime soon. Why? Bad things happen.

There's no way around it. Sometime, some place, some way, something bad happens to us all. Sorry to be the bearer of bad news.

Then again, we're pretty sure you already know that. You live life. You deal with people at school dishing out disses and meanness every day. And you hear the news. Headlines are always reminding us that bad stuff happens: "Cyberbullying on the Rise," "Tornado Tears Through Town," "Plane Goes Down." It's almost enough to make you want to hide in your closet. (Just don't watch the news nonstop; it'll depress you.) But there's a better way than that—a much better way. Keep reading.

HOW DO YOU HANDLE PROBLEMS?

People handle problems and challenges differently. How about you? Are you a sky-is-falling kind of person or a look-at-the-cool meteor-shower kind of person? Not sure? Which of these statements best describes you?

- Bad things? Whatever. They won't happen to me or the people I love.

- I guess bad things can happen, but I don't think about it much.

- Some bad stuff happens to everyone, so I keep a good life foundation: family, friends, and faith to get me through.

- I get worried and do everything I can to make sure nothing bad happens to me.

- I'm so busy worrying about what bad things might happen that I can't really think about what good things might happen.

There are probably lots of reasons why you chose your answer—and why you feel the way you do. Your personality, relationships, beliefs about God, past experiences, and current situation in life all play a part. But if your outlook isn't too positive, you can change it! You can get a grip on the reality that stuff happens in life by working on building a solid foundation in your life that brings strength, security, and hope. And you can find out firsthand that God is bigger than any badness that could ever come your way.

THE IMPACT ZONE

When things are going well, life can feel easy and perfect and like it will stay that way forever. But in less than an eye blink, a perfect day can turn into a bad dream. And when we are living life, especially life to the fullest by pursuing our dreams, we have to acknowledge the risks. We don't have to let them stop us, though.

At the beginning of the movie *Soul Surfer*, Bethany Hamilton says, "Life's an adventure, but sometimes you end up in the impact zone."

You can get a grip on the reality that stuff happens in life by working on building a solid foundation in your life that brings strength, security, and hope.

The what? The *impact zone* in surfing gives us a perfect example of the blow bad things can land—and the ability to get through them. The impact zone is exactly where surfers don't want to be. It's where the waves come down. And the bigger the wave, the harder the explosion when its lip slams back down into the ocean.

If you ever watch surfers, you'll notice they want to stay just in front of the curtain of water that's falling back down from the lip of the wave—or in a perfect ride on a big-enough wave, inside the hollow tube that's behind that breaking curtain. Can you picture it?

But if surfers bail off their boards, they can end up in the impact zone, in the area in front of all the breaking waves. It's a messy spot filled with whitewater foam and watery currents sucking back and forth. And because waves often come in sets of three or five or more, each one keeps pounding down on a floating surfer's head. Those waves pound surfers down deep underwater, tossing them like rag dolls. A surfer may be lucky enough to get to the surface for a breath of air before the next wave hits, but if not, things can get dangerous or even deadly.

Can you imagine what that would feel like? Actually, you probably can, because normal life has an impact zone too. And you've most likely been there. It blindsides you with a blast out of the blue. One minute you're riding along, minding your own business. The next minute, you're tumbling and turning and trying to figure out which end is up. Maybe it's when the guy or girl you've been crushing on suddenly starts treating you like you don't exist. Then your crush starts liking your best friend. Next thing you know, neither one of them will give you the time of day. Worse, your other friends quit talking to you, and you find out it's because someone has spread a rumor about you. You feel like you can barely catch a breath between these waves of rejection.

Or maybe your whole family gets caught in the impact zone. Maybe your dad or mom gets laid off from work. Then the bad starts slamming down. You have to move in the middle of the year. Or maybe your parents' fighting turns into—*Wait! What? Separating ... like divorce?* Your life feels like it's imploding with nuclear force.

That's the impact zone with wave after menacing wave, and it feels like it's never going to let you back up. It won't always be as drastic as these examples, but it doesn't have to be. No matter what your problems are, the feelings are the same—you feel alone, scared, out of control. You can go from the highest highs of living your passions and pursuing your dreams to feeling like life is pile driving you into the earth's core.

SO BAD HE'S FAMOUS

There's a guy in the Bible who felt like that. In fact, the circumstances of his life went wrong so fast that it's what he's famous for thousands of years later, even to people who don't read the Bible. His name was Job, with a long *o* as in "no way," not *job* like "Get a job."

Anyway, Job had a sweet life going before he got completely thrashed in life's impact zone. He was a good man. He loved his great family. He worked hard and was rich, especially when it came to sheep, goats, camels, donkeys, and oxen—that was like gold to people back then. But he had plenty of cash too. The Bible calls him *"the richest person in that entire area"* (Job 1:3 NLT). He also loved God and did everything right.

In fact, God even bragged on Job. "Check out Job," God said to the devil, though not exactly in these words. "He has got it going on! You want an example of how I want my humans to be? Job all the way. He's the best person on that whole planet down there."

The devil replies to God—again we're paraphrasing, "Well, duh. What do you expect? You give him everything he wants. Let me throw him around in the impact zone awhile, and we'll see how good he stays."

> **God pulled Job out of the impact zone and placed him in the God zone. He can do the same thing for us no matter what's going on in our lives.**

Here's some of what happens: Raiders attack and steal all Job's animals and kill all his servants. The house collapses and kills all ten of Job's kids. Finally, some nasty, itchy skin disease breaks out all over Job's body, and all he can do is sit and scratch his sores with broken pieces of pottery. Even his wife tells him he should give up.

But Job didn't. He hung on to God. He asked God a lot of questions and said, "God, this isn't fair. What's going on?" And God answered and told Job He was more powerful than any of Job's pain. Job continued trusting God. He wouldn't give up when it came to his faith. And God restored everything in Job's life. He even blessed Job with more of everything than he had started with: animals, money, children, and grandchildren.

God pulled Job out of the impact zone and placed him in the God zone. He can do the same thing for us no matter what's going on in our lives.

THE GOD ZONE

So what are you supposed to do with all this? What does God say about those curve balls life throws at us sometimes? Where is He in all that thrashing water?

Let's talk about that for a minute. He's right there with you. Every second. Every step. Every watery pitch and tumble!

In Psalm 32:7 of the Bible, we read the words of the King David (of David and Goliath fame). He had plenty of trouble—facing a menacing giant for one! He said this: "*You are my hiding place. You protect me from my troubles*" (NCV). That verse doesn't say you won't ever have problems. What it does say is that you won't ever have to face them alone. God Himself, the ruler of the whole big universe, has promised to protect you right there in the middle of the crashing waves and powerful currents. He won't let go of you—not ever. Once you have given Him your heart, there is nothing that can strip you out of His arms.

So why does trouble happen? Can't God keep all that bad stuff away? The Bible tells us a lot about that. But it's a question only God can answer completely. For now, it's enough to know He is on your side and He always will be. Nothing this world or even the devil and his forces of evil can devise is any match for Him. In Jeremiah 32:17 we read, "*Ah, Lord GOD! It is you who made the heavens and the earth by your great power and by your outstretched arm! Nothing is too hard for you*" (NRSV). When you put your hand in His hand, you are connecting with the almighty, all-powerful God. Once you are His, He will never let you go. How amazing is that?

Now, one more thing. Think about the impact zone with all that swirling, crashing water. Imagine how difficult it is for a surfer to stay calm in the middle of all that. And yet, that's pretty much the only way to conquer it. Give way to fear and panic and begin to fight against the wave, and you'll be in trouble for sure. But good surfers know to roll with it, to let the water propel them through it. They aren't afraid of the strength and power of the wave. Instead they use it to their advantage.

The same is true of life's impact zone. You must not let fear and panic overtake you. In the Bible, God instructs us, saying, "*God did not give us a spirit of timidity, but a spirit of power, of love and of self discipline.*" (2 Timothy 1:7). In the circumstance of life where you feel most fearful, God is saying to trust Him, His goodness, and His love for you. Roll with the difficult thing you are facing. Roll with it and let it propel you into a deeper faith in God. Let Him pull you up and out of the impact zone and into the God zone.

YOUR RIDE

Write five to ten news headlines for your life right now, maybe something like, "Girl Forgives After Fighting With Best Friend" or "Guy Able to Play Despite Broken Wrist." Include the good and the bad. Add some photos or draw some pictures to go along with your life headlines. Then write another five headlines about what God can do in the pain and happiness of your life.

"Do not fear the winds of adversity.
Remember: A kite rises against the wind
rather than with it."
—author unknown

"Search for the
seed of good in
every adversity."
—Og Mandino, author

"On days when life is difficult and I feel overwhelmed,
as I do fairly often, it helps to remember in my prayers
that all God requires of me is to trust Him and be His
friend. I find I can do that."
—Bruce Larson, pastor

"Adversity has the effect
of eliciting talents,
which in prosperous
circumstances would
have lain dormant."
—Horace, Roman poet

YOUR PLANS, GOD'S PLANS

"I've been trying to get some perspective. I've been really trying. ... But, Sarah, how could this be God's plan for me? I don't understand."

—Bethany Hamilton to Sarah Hill in the movie SOUL SURFER

One of the saddest scenes in the movie SOUL SURFER comes after the shark attack when Bethany goes to see her youth leader, Sarah Hill. Bethany loves God, and even though she has been trying hard to trust Him, she is struggling with the tragic loss of both her arm and her dream of becoming a professional surfer. None of it seems to make any sense. But even while she is suffering from pain and disappointment, Bethany is still trying to look at the bigger picture. Read what she says: "I've been trying to get some perspective."

Maybe you're having a time in your own life when your plans seem to be falling apart. You can still trust God's promises, and one of those promises is that He has His own plans for you—even when you can't see them. Let's take a look at some other people who exchanged their own plans for God's plans. Read on ...

Luma Mufleh came to the United States for a college education. Her wealthy family in Jordan could afford the best for their daughter, but they expected her to return after she graduated. Luma chose to stay, even though it meant that her father cut her off from the family. She turned her focus to owning her own restaurant. But years later, the restaurant she had sacrificed so much for was failing, and she found herself wondering what to do.

That's when she took a wrong turn while driving in Clarkston, Georgia, just outside of Atlanta. There, she spotted many international people wearing clothes like they did in her home country of Jordan. She also spotted a group of boys playing soccer barefoot in an apartment parking lot.

Sometimes, even when our plans seem good and right, God has other plans, bigger and better plans, in mind.

Luma returned a few days later with a new ball and asked if she could play. The boys agreed, and she began to learn their stories. They were refugees from Sudan, Afghanistan, Congo, Serbia, and all over the world. Their families had been relocated and thrown into American life in Clarkston. That's when Luma had a great idea. Start a team.

She quickly organized the team, which she called the Fugees (short for *refugees*) Family. All the boys were included, but Luma was strict. If the boys wanted to stay Fugees, they had to follow the rules, including doing well in school—not an easy job for some who could barely speak English—and staying away from the gangs and drugs in the area. But the boys didn't mind. The team gave them an identity in their new country. They put aside their cultural cliques and different languages and truly became a team and a family. They found something to believe in and work for.

What started as a "wrong turn" brought Luma a new dream and purpose—and it got even bigger than the soccer field.

Coach Luma got to know her players' families. They had escaped wars and terrible problems in their homelands, but they now faced the challenges of overcoming poverty. Luma helped them get enough food to eat. She helped mothers find jobs. She helped them fill out important forms and understand American ways. She helped them find opportunities for a better life. Luma and the Fugees found a deep sense of family. Not a bad change of direction, was it?

THE BIG PICTURE

Plans are good, but they often get changed. Sometimes, they get changed because something unexpected happens—your parents decide to move to another city just when you make the football team, for example. But sometimes, good things also can cause you to change your plans—a new interest, an unexpected opportunity. That's what happened to Coach Luma with the Fugees.

That's also what happened to a sixth grader named Isabel Jones from Vancouver, Canada. She went with her parents on a trip to Africa. When she got home, she planned to slip quietly back into her life. But she couldn't shake the images of all the people she had met in Africa who lacked many things she considered basic necessities—like shoes! Her usual sixth-grade plans were soon altered to allow Isabel time to collect shoes. Soon her efforts came to the attention of Forward Edge International, which helped her send the shoes to people in twelve countries who desperately needed them.

Writer Mitch Albom found his plans changing when he visited Haiti to help out after the 2010 earthquake. He ended up running an orphanage there. You can imagine how unexpected that was!

But what about good interruptions. That happens too. So what should you do when *good* interruptions create a change of plans? That's when you need to step back for a moment and see if there's a bigger purpose in what's going on. Sometimes, even when our plans seem good and right, God has other plans, bigger and better plans, in mind. He can see the big picture, and He knows things you don't.

Have you ever watched a friend play a video game for the first time after you've already mastered it? You know all the cheats, secret weapons, and hidden levels. Your instructions might sound strange to your friend, but you know they work. You've discovered the master plan. You know what's around the next corner and what happens in the end. You're seeing that game like God sees our lives.

As much as you love your friend, God loves you more. He sees the path of your life from beginning to end. He understands what is really important and what isn't. He knows what it will take to achieve your dream and the best path to get there. Sometimes, that means changing your plans. It often feels strange, but He always knows best. Trust Him with your plans and don't resist when you see them changing. Surrender to Him as you feel

Him drawing you closer to Him. No one loves you more or wants more good things from you than God.

HARD TO CHANGE

Talk about plans changing! Think about Bethany. She was a surfer through and through. When she first lost her arm, she couldn't see how she would ever surf again. If she couldn't surf, she was no longer a surfer. And if she wasn't a surfer, then who was she? What about her dream?

Probably no one would have thought less of her if she had just walked away and given up on surfing. After all, how do you even get up on a board with just one arm? Bethany had to choose to trust in God's big picture—and she did just that.

Bethany chose to turn to God and see what He had to tell her about the situation. In the Bible, she found this promise. *"'I know the plans I have for you,' declares the LORD, 'plans to prosper you and not to harm you, plans to give you hope and a future'"* (Jeremiah 29:11). In fact, that Bible verse became a theme for Bethany's life. She couldn't imagine how her old dream could survive, and she couldn't imagine what her life would be without it, but she held tight to God's promise that He had a good plan for her life, even if she couldn't see or understand it yet.

That's an amazing message, isn't it? A message for you just as it was for Bethany. It's good for you to make plans and go for them. But you can't lose sight of the fact that God may have bigger plans in the works for you. His plans are higher, deeper, and wider than any you can imagine; and He wants to work with you to make them happen.

His plans are higher, deeper, and wider than any you can imagine; and He wants to work with you to make them happen.

CHALLENGE OR GOD

Emily has planned and dreamed of singing and dancing—maybe on Broadway—since she was a little girl. She goes to every tryout for every school musical, play, and choir. But she can't seem to get a lead part. She ends up in the chorus every time. She doesn't understand. How will she ever make it to Broadway? Is this a challenge she should work hard to overcome? Or is this God trying to point her in a different direction? Is it possible that God has a better plan for Emily than the bright lights of Broadway?

Jared's passion is art. He has always sketched, painted, and drawn on every blank surface in sight. He's planning and dreaming of becoming an animator for Disney or DreamWorks someday. He just knew it would happen—until he started volunteering with an art mission in his city to help disadvantaged kids learn art skills and use them to deal with their difficult lives. Jared is a natural. He loves helping other kids and seeing creativity come alive in them. Could it be that God has a more fulfilling plan, a more lasting legacy for Jared than making animated films?

When life circumstances seem to interrupt your plans—especially when you're just starting to figure out your dreams and plans—how can you tell if it's just a challenge to overcome or God asking you to follow Him in a new direction? Sometimes, the answer is obvious. Other times, you won't know until you walk a little farther down life's road. And sometimes, it's not one or the other but both.

New doors and ways to use and engage gifts can spark new plans that bring you more alive inside than you could ever imagine.

Here are some questions to ask yourself when you begin to see your plans changing:

1. What new direction or greater good could come from this?

You've heard of Mary and Joseph—you know, the parents of Jesus. Those two young people suddenly found themselves in the middle of a plan that was way bigger than the two of them. They already had their own plans going—get married, live a good life together in a small town, and have a family. But then, angels started appearing. One told Mary, a virgin, that she was going to have a baby, God's Son.

She was more than a little surprised, but you know how the story goes. She said, "Okay, I'll trust You on this, God." Joseph agreed too, when an angel gave him the message also. And they eventually ended up in the stable in Bethlehem, where Mary gave birth to baby Jesus.

Mary didn't waste a minute holding on to her old plans. She could see right away that she'd been offered an amazing opportunity. She quickly and joyfully accepted that God wanted her to be part of a bigger, much more important plan—even though at the time she couldn't see how it would all work out.

Your turn: New doors and ways to use and engage gifts can spark new plans that bring you more alive inside than you could ever imagine. Be willing to explore and discover new and better plans.

2. Does my original plan include anything wrong, like cheating, lying, or compromising my purity?

Marlise Kast had come a long way from her conservative home and small Christian liberal arts college. At twenty-one, she was manipulating her way to deals and deception to get the scoop on Hollywood stars as a tabloid reporter for *Globe* magazine. It all started with the adrenaline rush of getting the story, but Marlise was soon compromising her values and integrity for a shot at hitting it big. She did too, writing more than two hundred articles for the tabloids. But God had other plans for Marlise that didn't involve compromised integrity.

Finally, after a dangerous high-speed chase and a big betrayal, Marlise was faced with a story she couldn't write—her conscience wouldn't let her. She left the world of the paparazzi and walked through a journey of discovering who she was outside of the lies and false identities. God led Marlise to use her passion for writing to write articles and books about travel and action sports.

Your turn: Following God's general guidelines in the Bible will help you hear and understand His best plans for your life. Is there any wrong thing you know of that's getting in your way?

3. Is this a detour or a delay?

Dan Jansen followed his passion, put his talents to use, pursued his dream, and made his plan. And it all took him to the 1988 Olympics. The speed skater was one of the gold-medal favorites for the 500 meters. He

What might look like a crazy detour to you can be God's road to your greatest dreams.

was ready to win. But on the day of the race, Dan got a call from his family. His sister, who had been extremely sick with leukemia, was dying. Dan talked with her over the phone and told her, "I love you." Six hours later, he found out she had died. Nothing was the same. He didn't feel like skating, but he raced because he knew how important his dream had been to his sister. He fell on the first turn and covered his head with his hands. Four days later, he raced again. This time, he was on a world-record pace about halfway through when he fell to the ice again and didn't finish the race.

What happened to Dan is understandable. He could have given up on his dream. But he didn't. He recognized that sometimes life gets in the way of our plans and dreams. He took time to be sad about losing his sister, but he kept skating. He won world championships, set new records, and went to the 1992 Olympics. Once again, his performance was disappointing. He finished nowhere near the medal platform. But even this second setback couldn't steal away his determination to reach his goal. He kept skating and returned again to the 1994 Olympics. His first race was going well until he slipped on the final turn. He caught himself but finished eighth. He had one race left—the 1,000 meters. He skated hard. He slipped but regained his balance, and he crossed the finish line with a new world record and a long-time-coming gold medal.

Dan Jansen had plenty of opportunities to give up. He could have decided that an Olympic medal just wasn't in the plans for him. But speed skating was his passion. And he was good at it. He remained one of the best in the world. He kept running into roadblocks when it came to winning Olympic medals, but there was no doubt he deserved to be there competing. It took years, but Dan finally achieved his dream.

Your turn: It can take a lot of work and a lot of time to achieve a dream. Waiting and pushing through a lot of disappointments might be part of the picture. But God wants you to keep working and keep believing until you get there. Unless, of course, you realize God has a bigger and better plan in mind for you.

LOOKING BACK

By now you may be thinking, *Great, I'm part of a bigger picture. My plans might work out in time. But how do I know God's plans are always good ones?*

First of all, because God is good and He loves us. Jesus proved how much God loves all of us by dying for us on the cross. So great and immeasurable is His love that the Bible tells us He *is* love. And He wants to prove it to us if we'll let Him.

You can start by looking back. It's what God told His people, the Israelites, to do when they were having trouble trusting. He more or less said, "Hey, remember all the ways I took care of you in the past? Remember when my plans looked weird but worked out better than you imagined? I can and will do it again."

Can you think of times in your life so far when God's plans were different from yours? Maybe something happened that completely changed your plans, and you had nothing to say about it. Or maybe you felt like God was asking you to give something up—maybe your dream took a change of direction. How did it all turn out? How did you react? What did you learn?

Maybe you've never experienced what it's like to put your plans or your life in God's hands. Maybe you've just started to figure out what your plans and dreams are. Either way, try turning over your passions and dreams to the Master Planner. Turn to Him as you navigate the roadblocks and detours. He wants to guide you along the way.

Talk to friends and family too, and ask them to tell you their stories of how God worked His plan for good in their lives. Their stories can be a big encouragement when your plans seem cloudy or confused.

So go ahead and make your plans. You need them to give you a way to reach your dream. But hold them loosely. Always keep doing your best, but when you feel your fist tightening around your plan, remind yourself to open your hand and loosen your grip—and turn to God for help. Remember, *"You can make many plans, but the LORD's purpose will prevail"* (Proverbs 19:21 NLT). What might look like a crazy detour to you can be God's road to your greatest dreams.

YOUR RIDE

Draw yourself a road map of life. It could look like a road or a timeline or navigational system directions. Show some places you were headed and some you are headed to now. Mark some landmarks along the way—places where you took a new turn or where someone or something changed your route. Be creative. It's your map. Use it to visualize where God might be leading you now.

N

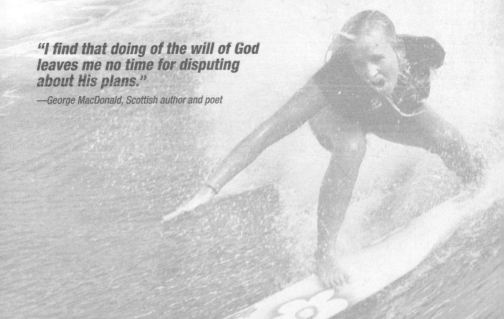

Allow your dreams a place in your prayers and plans. God-given dreams can help you move into the future He is preparing for you.

– Barbara Johnson, author

When one door of happiness closes, another opens; but often we look so long at the closed door that we do not see the one which has been opened to us.

– Helen Keller, deaf and blind author

"I find that doing of the will of God leaves me no time for disputing about His plans."

—George MacDonald, Scottish author and poet

CHAPTER 9
IT HURTS SO BAD

"You're going to be in a lot of pain because of the trauma you've endured."

–Dr. Rovinsky to Bethany Hamilton in the movie SOUL SURFER

In the movie SOUL SURFER, *when Bethany wakes up in the hospital, the first things she tells her parents is, "It hurts." Maybe when you watched that scene, you thought,* Wow, I bet it does! *Bethany had just gone through an incredibly scary, shocking, and yes ... painful experience. When Dr. Rovinsky arrives in Bethany's room, he explains to her that the pain is normal and expected.*

Most of us think that pain simply hurts, but did you ever consider that it might keep you safe? Keep reading, and you'll learn why pain can be a necessary and even important part of life.

If you were granted three wishes from a genie in a bottle and one of those wishes was that you would never feel pain again, would you imagine that to be a good thing or a bad thing? You may be saying, "Hot diggity! No more toothaches, muscle aches, cold sores, stomach cramps, skinned elbows and knees—wow! That would be totally awesome!" Or would it?

Ashlyn Blocker's parents were stoked when they brought her home from the hospital. They had a precious new baby girl, and she was an angel! Hungry? No crying. Gas pains? No problem. Diaper rash? Not a peep. It was great—until they began to realize that their daughter wasn't just a happy baby; something was wrong. They soon learned that Ashlyn suffers from a rare genetic disorder called congenital insensitivity to pain. She doesn't feel pain or the extremes of hot or cold. She is one of fewer than twenty documented cases in the United States.

The no-pain thing was great when diaper rash flared up. But it was no good when Ashlyn scratched the surface of her cornea. Her parents only discovered it when they took her to the doctor after her bloodshot eye didn't get better with drops. When Ashlyn began teething, she would chew her lips until they bled and bite through her tongue when she ate.

The risks got even greater as she got older and more independent. When she was three, Ashlyn seriously injured her hand by touching a hot pressure washer. She didn't cry—she was just fascinated by her red, blistered hand. Every day at school provided multiple injury opportunities for the girl with no fear, from the jungle gym to the hot soup served in the cafeteria.

The Blockers have done all they can to make Ashlyn's life in Patterson, Georgia, as normal as possible. They've taken precautions, educated the people who care for her, and taught Ashlyn to recognize the signs of pain. If she sees blood, she knows to stop and get help.

Ashlyn and her family would be quick to say that pain is a very important part of life.

DIFFERENT KINDS OF HURTS

What's the worst pain you've ever felt? Toothache? Stomachache? Broken bone? Hand slammed in a car door? Or maybe your worst pain is a different kind—an inside pain, a broken heart. Maybe your family split apart or a loved one died. Or maybe a friend betrayed you so badly that you felt like a crushed tin can inside. That old saying "sticks and stones can break my bones, but words can never hurt me" is a lie. Words can hurt a lot!

Yep! Nobody likes to be in pain. But if you can open your mind to the possibility, you might have to agree that pain can also be a friend. If you're willing to face it and learn to deal with it, pain can help you see a deeper meaning in life. Pain can point you to the Healer—God. And pain can make you stronger than you ever thought you could be. Let's think for a moment about what pain teaches us.

If you're willing to face it and learn to deal with it, pain can help you see a deeper meaning in life.

He wants to pour out His love and compassion on you.

GOOD PAIN

Physical pain teaches us not to touch a hot stove or reach into a fireplace ever again. Emotional pain can teach us to stay away from unhealthy relationships and unwise choices, because last time they burned us on the inside. Mental and emotional pain can teach us how to focus our priorities and where to turn for comfort and healing.

What's your favorite movie? Now identify what kind of pain the main character faced. The main character always has some kind of painful circumstance to overcome. In chick flicks, the pain or problem is usually emotional, some misunderstanding or lack of a relationship (and, of course, it takes a heroic prince to rescue the girl or declare his love for her). In action films, the pain or suffering is most often physical, an enemy trying to kill the hero or destroy the earth (and, of course, it takes lots of explosives and car chases to solve the problem).

A story without some kind of tension, conflict, pain, or dramatic crisis is just plain boring. And life is the same way. A guy named Donald Miller wrote a whole book about this idea called *A Million Miles in a Thousand Years*. He looked at his life and asked, "Am I living a good story?" He tried to imagine what he would think if he were reading about himself as a character. He tried to make choices that a book or movie hero might make in living an adventurous life. And he realized that people can't successfully chase their dreams unless they are willing to risk some pain or hardship to do it. When the focus of life is to avoid discomfort, we are not riding the adventure of God's wave.

BETTER THAN THE ALTERNATIVE

Sometimes, avoiding pain at all costs can actually cost us our lives. Just ask Aron Ralston, whose story is told in a movie called *127 Hours*. Here's the short version. Aron hiked alone into the Utah desert to do some trekking, climbing, and rappelling through the desert's narrow slot canyons. A loose thousand-pound boulder fell and wedged against the canyon wall with Aron's arm underneath it. Ouch. So he could just call for help or wait for help to come along, right? Wrong. Aron was in the middle of nowhere. No phone. Nobody within miles. And he hadn't told anyone where he was going.

Aron tried everything he could think of to move the rock. It wouldn't budge. After five days, Aron knew he was going to die unless he did something drastic. He broke the bones in his lower arm. Then he sawed his arm off with his dull multitool. It worked. He was free. He still had to rappel down a sixty-five-foot cliff and hike eight miles back to his truck, but he finally met some other hikers and got help. And he lived.

Talk about pain! Aron said later that his self-amputation hurt a hundred times worse than any pain he'd ever felt before. But Aron knew he had to go through the pain to have any chance at surviving. Later on, he wrote in his blog, "A hand and forearm are not a life." In fact, Aron's life has been full since his ordeal. He still rock climbs using a prosthetic arm and does many other outdoor activities. He became a public speaker, got married, has a family, and Hollywood made a movie about his inspiring story. Aron has lived a full life on the other side of his most intense pain.

Don't get us wrong. We're not suggesting cutting off your arm. In fact, we're telling you: Do not cut off any limbs, unless you find yourself literally trapped in the wilderness for five days with absolutely no other option to free yourself.

And on a much more serious note, don't ever cut or purposefully injure yourself. Self-inflicted physical pain is not a way out of emotional pain. It's a harmful trap and a cheap substitute for real healing. It's not the kind of pain we're talking about in this book.

Even if cutting or burning or some other self-injury feels better at first, it only leads to worse addiction and depression. And it doesn't deal with your real pain on the inside. If you or someone you know is struggling with self-injury, reach out for help to a trusted adult, maybe a youth leader or teacher if you can't talk to your parents. Go to these two Web sites for help, resources, and understanding: To Write Love on Her Arms (twloha.org) and S.A.F.E. Alternatives (SelfInjury.com).

HOPE IN PAIN

In the beginning, God created everything exactly like He intended it to be: pure, good, and right. The first people, Adam and Eve, lived in a perfect paradise. But you know what happened: snake, fruit, temptation, sin. That perfect world became stained and damaged. Enter pain, suffering, sadness, and even death. Our direct connection with God was broken. And the Bible says it broke God's heart.

So when you find yourself asking questions like *Why, God?* and *Why me?* know that God is not the author of your pain. He takes no pleasure in it. That's why He sent Jesus into the world. Jesus became one of us, identifying with our pain and restoring our connection with our heavenly Father. When you give your heart to Him, you will once again be in close relationship with Him. Pain can no longer make you feel small and weak because you are hooked up to the greatest of all power sources, God Himself. And one day when God completes His ultimate work, things will once again be as God intended them: perfect, pure, and filled with light.

No matter what pain you encounter, remember this: Running to God with your pain isn't running away from it. You are running for help to the One who understands perfectly; He wants to pour out His love and compassion on you. He's the best solution for any pain you'll ever encounter.

YOUR RIDE

What is your story? What tension, conflict, pain, or dramatic crisis is going on in your life? Write the story of your life. Include the pain you're experiencing and script the ending that you can't yet see in real life. How can you conquer your pain? What can you achieve? What's your happy ending? Are you connected to God and experiencing His hope and victory? What choices in real life can you make to put you in the flow of His love, comfort, and unlimited resources?

If you really want to get into this exercise, get out your video camera and make it into a movie.

"Difficult times have helped me to understand better than before, how infinitely rich and beautiful life is in every way."
—Isak Dinesen, author of Out of Africa

"We cannot learn without pain."
—*Aristotle, philosopher*

"You may never know that Jesus is all you need, until Jesus is all you have."
—Corrie ten Boom, Holocaust survivor and author

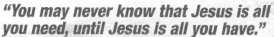

PART 4

Resurfacing

CATCHING GOD'S WAVE

Philippians 4:4

Rejoice in the Lord always. I will say it again: Rejoice!

Nehemiah 8:10

"Do not grieve, for the joy of the LORD is your strength."

Matthew 6:34

Therefore do not worry about tomorrow, for tomorrow will worry about itself. Each day has enough trouble of its own.

Colossians 3:23

Whatever you do, work at it with all your heart, as working for the Lord.

Ephesians 4:23 AMP

Be constantly renewed in the spirit of your mind [having a fresh mental and spiritual attitude]...

1 Thessalonians 5:11

Therefore encourage one another and build each other up, just as in fact you are doing.

CHAPTER 10

ATTITUDE ADJUSTMENT

**"You were amazing out there. You were the one
who kept me calm, and you never let go. You are
incredibly brave, Bethany."**

—Holt Blanchard to Bethany Hamilton in the movie SOUL SURFER

In the movie SOUL SURFER, *the shark-attack scene is totally intense. The
shark has come out of nowhere and shattered the beauty and peace of the
morning. Bethany has lost her arm. There's blood pouring into the water, and
the surfers have to somehow make it back over the reef and up the hill to the
truck before Bethany loses her life. That kind of scene would make anyone
lose their cool! But in the midst of it all, Bethany remains calm, helps paddle
in to shore, and calls on her best chance to live by praying, "Please, Jesus,
please, get me to the beach."*

*Why do some people become bitter and angry in the face of trouble, and
others seem courageous and strong? It's all about attitude! In this chapter,
we're going to meet some people whose attitudes have helped them climb out
of difficulties and up into the God zone. Read on ...*

Nick Vujicic (pronounced *vooy-cheech*) had a hard time when he was a
teenager. He had to deal with bullies. He struggled with his self-esteem.
And mostly, he had to live every second of every day with no arms and no

legs. That's the way Nick was born. There was no medical explanation. His arms and legs just didn't grow.

Can you even imagine what that would mean? No giving hugs. No holding hands. No combing your hair or brushing your teeth. No walking, running, jumping, or dancing. No wonder Nick had trouble accepting who he was. On the inside, the Australian was just like every one of us, but on the outside, he looked very different.

Nick's faith in God kept him holding on. He figured out that he couldn't do anything to change his body, but he could change the way he chose to think about and deal with his disability. By the time he was nineteen, Nick began to tell his story to others. That's when he found his purpose and passion in life, and he embraced it. Now Nick has spoken all over the world. He runs his own nonprofit organization called Life Without Limbs and a motivational-speaking company called Attitude is Altitude. He has inspired millions. "If God can use a man without arms and legs to be His hands and feet, then He will certainly use any willing heart!" he says.

ONE THING

Do you remember what we said about the impact zone? That is, how important it is to stay calm, not to panic, and to let the power of the water propel you to where you need to be. Great surfers know they can't control the water, but they can choose to roll with it and let it work for them.

It's also true that you can't control many of the circumstances of your life, but you can choose how you deal with those circumstances. You can choose to commit yourself to God and let Him pull you up into the God zone. That's all about *attitude*! In any and every circumstance in life, you get to make one choice: How will you respond to what is going on around you?

So what's your attitude when you face life's daily hardships? How do you respond when a teacher gives you a grade you don't deserve, or a friend turns on you, or

You can find hope to face tomorrow in God's invitation to come swim in the deep sea of His love.

you get injured right before the big soccer game? Sure, it's easy to feel like a victim when painful things happen. But why choose to focus on what's wrong when you can choose instead to be hopeful and take a positive outlook? Why would you just take it when you can put yourself and your troubles in God's hands and let Him pull you into the God zone? Why settle for being a victim when you can be a victor by trusting God!

The Bible tells us that *"in all these things we are more than conquerors through him who loved us"* (Romans 8:37). What kind of "all these things" is this verse talking about? It means your struggles, your challenges, and the obstacles between you and your dream. In other words, you can be a conqueror even when you feel like life is conquering you! Why? Because the all-powerful God of the universe is with you. You don't have to face your struggles alone. He loves you and He is always there for you. Nothing that has happened, is happening, or will happen to you can ever tear you away from Him. You can find hope to face tomorrow in God's invitation to come swim in the deep sea of His love. And when you do, you will find a hope that's bigger than your problems and pain. You can find a strength to face them, knowing that God will carry you through whatever you're facing. You can find a focus that changes your attitude.

"If I allow pain to make me bitter, it blinds me to the truth of what God wants to do in my life," said Martin Luther, the famous Christian leader from the Middle Ages. Bitterness is where we land if we look away from God, pointing ourselves in the opposite direction. When we only focus on our pain, we get sucked into its black hole of bitterness. And bitterness is like cancer that eats us up inside.

Have you ever seen pictures of cataracts on people's or animals' eyes? They look like cloudy calluses on the eyeballs. They gradually make vision fuzzier and fuzzier. Bitterness works the same way. It takes over

When you find yourself stuck in the trap of asking why me?, ask a better question. Ask, what now?

your attitude and outlook and turns it darker and darker until there's no hope left in sight.

But there's great news! It doesn't have to be that way. You have a choice. You can choose discouragement and a dismal outlook, or you can choose to say no to bitterness, kick discouragement out the door, blast that dismal outlook, and put all your trust in the God who loves you so very much. The Bible tells us that the great King David made his choice during a painful time in his life. He said, *"Why are you down in the dumps, dear soul? Why are you crying the blues? Fix my eyes on God—soon I'll be praising again. He puts a smile on my face. He's my God"* (Psalm 42:11, MSG).

Turn your focus on God. You can lean on Him. He'll take care of you, and He'll help you reach your dream. After all, He's the one who gave it to you in the first place, right?

TWENTY QUESTIONS

Have you ever played the game Twenty Questions? It won't win the "Most Entertaining Game of the Year" award, but it's great when you're stuck in the car on a long road trip and the batteries are dead in all your electronic gadgets. Just in case you haven't played this classic, here's how it goes:

The first player thinks up an object. The second player gets to ask yes or no questions—twenty of them—to figure it out. The kind of questions you ask will make or break you in this game. If you start off making wild, random guesses, you won't have much chance. But if you start broad and narrow down your questions, your chances are way better.

The quality of real-life questions we ask when we're going through a hard time is important too. Thankfully, they don't have to be yes or no questions! The most common first question when we're nailed by pain is *Why?* It's natural. We want to make sense of the situation and find a reason in it. But even though *Why?* is often the first question asked, it's usually the last one answered. So instead of getting frustrated, we should work on asking better questions. Think of it this way: When you're stuck in the ocean's impact zone, it doesn't help much to ask why the waves are pounding or why they're "picking on" you. The right questions are, How do I relax and not waste oxygen? How do I get up for air? How do I swim out of this spot? And is there anyone around to help?

Do you see the difference? Try some of these questions for real life:

- Does this situation kill my dream?

- Does this situation change how I go after my dream?

- What have I lost?

- What do I still have?

- Who else has gone through something like this?

- What kind of doors can this situation open for me?

- When can I start pursuing those opportunities?

- What do I need to do to make it through today?

- What can I learn from God in this situation?

- What is hardest about this for me?

- Who is best able to help me right now?

- How does my situation impact other people?

- Is there anyone I should be helping?

That's not actually twenty questions, but we wanted to leave some for you to ask. What are some good questions you can ask about something hard you're going through?

And if you're willing to ride God's wave for your life, these activities can turn you toward God's bigger picture.

_____

_____

_____

STAYING POSITIVE

When you find yourself stuck in the trap of asking why me?, ask a better question. Ask, what now? That's the question that will pull you out of self-pity and get you looking ahead and moving toward a positive attitude. But an attitude is more than just a frame of mind. It's an expression of what's inside. Why do you think your mom tells you, "Don't give me that attitude"? She can tell by your tone of voice, actions, speech, expressions, even gestures that things inside you aren't right.

One way to help adjust your attitude is to do some positive activity that will jump-start positive feelings inside. The activity doesn't have to be superdeep or meaningful. Sometimes, it's better if it's not. The whole purpose is to help take your focus off yourself and put it on something positive. Here are some ideas:

- Run a mile.
- Clean the bathroom.
- Call a friend.
- Read a book.
- Clean out your closet.
- Cook a good meal.
- Watch a sunset.
- Do your homework.
- Go to a concert.

- Play with your dog.
- Mow the yard.
- Visit the zoo.
- Ride a bike.
- Shoot hoops.
- Paint a picture.
- Jam on your instrument.

Now add a few of your own ideas:

_____

_____

_____

_____

None of these activities will answer all your questions or heal your pain, but they can remind you of the rest of your life. They can transport you away from bitterness. They can help you remember what you still have and help you trust that things will get better again. They can blow on the embers of your heart's passion and remind you of your dream. They can help you reach out for the What now? And if you're willing to ride God's wave for your life, these activities can turn you toward God's bigger picture. They can remind you that God's plan is worth waiting for.

Surround yourself with people who keep life balanced and like to laugh and make you laugh.

LAUGH ON!

Here's another question for you. Do you like to laugh and have a good time with your friends? Of course you do. But did you know it's also good medicine when you're hurting and a good way to adjust your attitude?

The Bible says, *"A cheerful heart is good medicine"* (Proverbs 17:22). Now science is proving that it's true. Doctors and scientists at the Mayo Clinic now say that laughter can stimulate your heart, lungs, and muscles. It can help your body take in more oxygen, trigger the release of endorphins (those are your body's natural painkillers that make you feel good), relieve stress, and lower blood pressure. Laughter can even ease pain and improve your immune system. That's some powerful stuff!

So keeping a good sense of humor even in the middle of a painful situation can be a big help. It can really help to adjust your attitude. Surround yourself with people who keep life balanced and like to laugh and make you laugh. Watch a funny movie. Tell jokes. Keep laughing!

BETTER DAYS AHEAD

Don't you get excited when you've got something to look forward to? You could probably hardly sleep before Christmas when you were little. Now you might count down the days to the end of school or a school dance.

Well, you've got something to look forward to now. No matter what's going on in your life, you've got better days coming. How can we be so sure? Did you know that the Bible tells us, *"We know that God causes everything to work together for the good of those who love God and are called according to his purpose for them"* (Romans 8:28, NLT). Did you catch those key words? *Everything* and *good*. Those are ginormously important. God can take every single thing in life, pain included, and make something good out of it—somehow, some way, sometime.

No matter how bad you feel, take one step toward rejecting bitterness and discouragement and embracing positive feelings of hope and trust in God. Those feelings aren't based on empty promises. Ask God to prove Romans 8:28 in your life. He can and He will!

YOUR RIDE

The book of Psalms in the Bible is filled with some real emotions. The writers (primarily that King David guy again) weren't afraid to get honest and pour out their feelings to God. It didn't make their problems disappear, but they did discover new hope as they focused on God and His goodness, faithfulness, and love.

Try this: read Psalm 27:7–14 and Psalm 57. (If you don't have a Bible, you can look them up online at BibleGateway.com.) Then write your own psalm here. Think of it as a poem, song, journal, or prayer—just use your words to get it all out. Then choose to trust that God is going to help you through this problem or difficulty.

"The best cure is to find someone else's feet to wash, but failing that, washing almost anything will do."

—Barbara Brown Taylor, author and priest

"Bad things do happen; how I respond to them defines my character and the quality of my life. I can choose to sit in perpetual sadness, immobilized by the gravity of my loss, or I can choose to rise from the pain and treasure the most precious gift I have—life itself."

—Walter Anderson, German ethnologist

"What is the difference between an obstacle and an opportunity? Our attitude toward it. Every opportunity has a difficulty, and every difficulty has an opportunity."

—J. Sidlow Baxter, author and pastor

"Sometimes the Lord rides out the storm with us and other times He calms the restless sea around us. Most of all, He calms the storm inside us in our deepest inner soul."

—Lloyd John Ogilvie, former chaplain of the US senate

CHAPTER 11

TIME TO HEAL

"It's looking great. It's healing nicely."

–Dr. Rovinsky to Bethany Hamilton in the movie SOUL SURFER

In the movie SOUL SURFER, Bethany has to visit Dr. Rovinsky so he can remove her bandages and allow her arm to heal. It's a tough scene because Bethany has to again confront the reality of her missing arm. Even with surgery, the shark attack has left behind stitches and a scar. Dr. Rovinsky was able to operate on Bethany's arm, but how do you put a bandage on disappointment? What kind of ointment do you use to heal broken dreams? In this movie scene, Bethany's arm is healing, but she also has the tough challenge of mending her heart.

Have you ever suffered a big injury or gone through a long illness? What about losing a dream or getting dumped by a girlfriend or boyfriend? There are a lot of times in life when we have to go through a healing process. In this chapter, you'll read about how you can recover from both physical and emotional wounds in life.

You've heard those amazing stories, the ones about somebody lifting a car off of someone who's pinned underneath it from an accident? Or the one about a mother who wrestled a seven-hundred-pound polar bear to protect her kids? (This seriously happened.) Or Bethany Hamilton remaining amazingly calm even after she was attacked by a shark. Science can't totally explain these things. But in a moment of crisis, our adrenaline and instinct kick in and make us able to do things we never thought possible.

Too bad the burst of strength doesn't last. If it did, we could all be superheroes. In real life, once the crisis is over, there's a healing that has to happen. You see it on your body with the simplest cut or scrape. It takes a while to scab over and go away.

Healing on the inside is the resurfacing this part is talking about. It's filling your lungs with air after getting thrashed around in the impact zone. It's getting back to your life and your dreams. It's when you start to ask questions like *What now?* and take your first baby steps toward recovery.

Check out Olympic gymnast Kerri Strug. It was the 1996 Olympics in Atlanta, Georgia, and the US women were determined to win their first-ever team gold medal. They started strong, building a big lead, but began to falter in the final rotation of events. With the Russians catching up to them, it all came down to Kerri Strug and her final vault.

The four-foot nine teen sprinted down the runway and launched into a Yurchenko (any vault that begins with a roundoff back handspring) with a one-and-a-half twist. Sound difficult? It is. Kerri slipped on the landing, fell on her rear, and heard a pop. She had torn two ligaments in her ankle. Normally that would be a competition ender, but Kerri knew her score was only 9.162, not enough to be sure of gold. She also knew she had another vault coming. But could she do it? She had to try. After all, this was the Olympics. She had been working toward her dream of a gold medal for as long as she could remember.

"Please, God, help me make this vault," she prayed, as her coach helped her to the starting line. She looked down the seventy-five-foot runway, took a deep breath, and ran with all her might. The Russians stopped to watch. Once again Kerri leaped, vaulted, flew, and twisted. This time she came down flat on her feet. She heard another pop. She raised her injured foot off the ground and straightened up with her hands over her head. She forced a smile, held her landing long enough for the judges, and then collapsed on the mat. The crowd went quiet as her coach and teammates rushed to her. Kerri was carried off on a stretcher that day, but not before she saw the scoreboard: K Strug 9.712. Gold medal for the United States!

It's filling your lungs with air after getting thrashed around in the impact zone.

What a victory! All America took notice. Kerri was treated like a hero. Her picture was posted on Wheaties boxes. She visited all the big television shows. But she had badly damaged tendons in her ankle. Kerri faced a long healing process. In fact, it took nine months for the injury to fully heal.

HARD TO GO HOME

Hospitals don't heal injuries; they just get you well enough to survive when you go home. It's hard to go home after an injury or illness. The hospital is such a protected place with people who understand and give you all kinds of support. But there comes a time when you have to go back to real life.

You're not yet healed. But you're no longer in crisis either. This is the point when your emotions can catch up with you. The risk of infection is low, but the risk of depression is high. Your body has taken a blow, and your soul probably has too. This is when your plans look derailed. You made it out of the impact zone, but you're shaky and weak. You're having a hard time knowing if God is redirecting your dream or telling you this one is all done.

Add any scenario you want, and it's similar. Maybe you've found yourself in one of these:

You go through a breakup with a boyfriend or girlfriend. You might even be the one to end the relationship and want to go in a new direction. But then you start feeling lonely and missing your ex. You might be tempted to wonder, *What was I thinking?* You were strong in the breakup, but now you've got a lot of hard feelings to deal with. You need time to heal.

Or someone close to you dies. It's a terrible blow. You're sad and in shock. In the first few days, lots of friends and family are around to support you and remember the person you've lost. Then the relatives go home, and you have to get back to real life. But you really miss your loved one, and life doesn't seem the same without them. Your healing has just begun.

In any case, back to life means back to reality. It's returning to what you knew before except everything, including you, has changed. You have to find small ways, one day at a time, to re-create life in your new reality.

A TIME TO HEAL

How do you re-create life in your new reality? That's the big question. Here are some ideas as you begin to take those baby steps forward:

- *Keep worry under control.* Worry is like the black gooey sludge from an oil spill. Once it creeps into your mind and heart, it spreads all over everything. The best way to stop worry is to stop it as soon as it starts. Try the activities we talked about in the last chapter to clear your mind. And most important, take your worries to God. The Bible promises He'll replace your worries with His supernatural peace that will calm you inside and out (see Philippians 4:6–7).

- *Live today.* When you're healing, it's easy to get ahead of yourself. You start trying to figure out how you're going to climb a mountain when you can barely walk to the bathroom. That doesn't mean you can't work toward tomorrow; it just means you shouldn't let it stop you from living today. Refocus on your dream and ask God to show you what you can do *today* to get closer to achieving it.

- *Take it slow.* Be patient—healing takes time. Emotional healing is harder to see, but emotional scars often take longer to heal than physical ones. You won't have it all figured out right away, so let yourself ease back into life. Don't make your injuries worse by rushing it. Give yourself time to heal correctly.

- *Try something new.* During the healing process, you may not be able to do some of the things you love. That makes it a good time to try something new. It might even help you decide which dreams to keep going after.

- *Allow yourself to fail.* The only way to move ahead is to try. Think of babies when they learn to walk. They barely get vertical and then— boom! they topple over. Does it stop them? No way. Up and down they go ... again and again. And eventually, they get it. If babies quit trying, they'd still be sitting on their diapers. If Thomas Edison had given up when he failed, we might still be burning candles or gas lamps. He invented the first practical incandescent lightbulb, but it took a while. He finally got it right on his ten-thousandth try!

- *Keep a journal.* Write down what you're going through. Look back every once in a while. Reading where you came from to get where you are now can encourage you with how much progress you've made. It's like dropping pins on a digital map. You can see how far you've come from one point to the next. Be honest. Be creative. Write to yourself. Write to God. Get out what's inside of you.

- *Reset your mood to positive.* You know how you love your music? It's a powerful medium that can pump you up and inspire you. It would be good to add some worship music to what you usually listen to. It will help you focus your attention on God, your powerful and compassionate Healer.

THE GREAT HEALER

Jesus was very busy when He was here on earth. Once He had chosen His disciples, they traveled about with Him as He taught multitudes of people about God. Most of His talks took place outdoors, and anyone who wanted to could stop and listen. No one was excluded. And Jesus did more than just talk. He followed up His lessons with actions. He blessed a small amount of food and used it to feed thousands of people. Sometimes, He healed those who were sick and hurting. No wonder the crowds kept coming. It didn't matter to Jesus what was wrong with them, He just touched them and healed them. The Bible is full of people who came to Jesus with big and small problems and walked away fully restored. It's pretty amazing stuff—miraculous stuff actually.

In chapter 2 of the book of Mark, there's a mind-bogglingly incredible story about how Jesus told a paralyzed guy to get up and walk—and he did!

This is the story in our own words. Four men had been listening to Jesus teach about God's love and compassion. They heard Him say that God is on our side and wants to be a loving heavenly Father to us. They also had seen Jesus touch people and heal them. As they listened, they remembered a friend who was leading a sad and hopeless life because he was paralyzed. They knew they had to do whatever they could to get their friend to Jesus.

The four men found their friend and carried him to the house where Jesus was teaching that day. But there was a problem. Jesus was in the house, and so many people were crowded inside with Him that the four men couldn't get their friend anywhere near the Teacher and Healer. Then one of them had an idea. He suggested they carry their friend up onto the roof, make a hole up there, and lower him down in front of where Jesus was sitting. It was a crazy idea for sure—but it worked! Jesus liked their faith and how hard they tried. He looked at the man with love and compassion and said, "Son, your sins are forgiven."

Can you picture the look on the men's faces when Jesus said that? The Bible doesn't tell us what they said, but they must have been surprised. They expected Jesus to touch their friend and make him walk again, but they weren't expecting Him to also heal him on the inside.

Jesus wanted everyone watching and listening to Him that day to know that He wants to heal our bodies *and* our hearts. That day, He began by healing the man on the inside, and then He healed his body, as well. Those four men must have been whooping and clapping as Jesus told their friend to stand up, pick up his mat, and walk, whole in body and soul. Then the Bible says the man did just that, and everyone watching was amazed and praising God, saying they had never seen anything like it.

What does that mean to you? It means you should never underestimate His ability to bring healing into your life. God wants to help you come to the place of asking *What now?* and looking forward to the new priorities and adventures He has for your life.

GAINING STRENGTH

Some healing is miraculously quick and complete (that's what the paralyzed man experienced). But in most cases, healing is more of a process. Bethany Hamilton would be the first to tell you that healing up often involves daily choices and hard work. It can feel like two steps forward, one step back. But when you keep walking through it with patience, you gain strength.

Have you ever lifted weights? It's the same concept. Lifting weights pushes our muscles to work harder than normal. It actually pushes them to the point of developing tiny microtears; your muscles get slightly damaged. Then as blood flows to them and the body repairs itself, the muscles are built back even stronger and bigger.

You'll get stronger too as you ride God's wave and live life to its fullest. You may just find you're able to conquer challenges others don't know how to face—like Nat Strand.

Nat was twelve when she found out she had type 1 diabetes. Her parents sent her to summer camp thinking she was a happy, healthy girl, but when she got home, they knew something was wrong. They rushed their daughter to the hospital where they discovered she had a disease that would impact the rest of her life.

In type 1 diabetes, the body doesn't produce *insulin*, a hormone needed to convert sugar, starches, and other food into energy for our daily lives. So diabetics have to constantly monitor their blood-sugar levels to avoid life-threatening situations. They have to inject insulin into their bodies to make sure they have enough to keep their bodies running. Nat's life, activities, and potential would all be forever affected and possibly limited by this disease. But instead of letting it hold her back, Nat learned and experienced all she could. Rather than asking, *Why me?* she asked, *What now?* She adjusted to her new reality in a way that moved her ahead in life.

Fast forward to age thirty-one. In 2010, Nat was a doctor. She and a fellow doctor competed in the reality-television show *The Amazing Race*. If you've seen the show, you know contestants have to travel around the world, face crazy physical challenges, and eat gross stuff. They only get to bring what they carry in a backpack from the start. Nat's pack was filled mostly with diabetic supplies, and she faced the extra challenge of constantly keeping her insulin levels under control. Not only did she manage to take care of herself, she and her teammate, Kat Chang, won! Want to know their winning strategy? It was something Nat started learning when she was twelve years old: "Never, never, never give up—never."

Sounds like good advice.

YOUR RIDE

Experiment time. Turn a faucet on so that it drips water out one drop at a time. Doesn't look like much, does it? Put a bucket underneath and leave it. Come back an hour later and see how much of the bucket is filled. Check again until it's all filled up.

This little object lesson is intended to remind you that healing often comes one step at a time, but God is in it. He wants to help you resurface after you come up out of the impact zone. Each day you get closer to being whole again. Be patient. God is good and His plans never fail. Take each step God reveals to you. That's all He asks. He will do the rest. Now, take your bucket and water a tree.

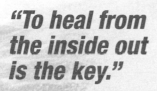

"Victory is won not in miles but in inches. Win a little now, hold your ground, and later, win a little more."
—Louis L'Amour, author

"Although the world is full of suffering, it is full also of the overcoming of it."
—Helen Keller, deaf and blind author

"Healing takes courage, and we all have courage, even if we have to dig a little to find it."
—Tori Amos, musician

"To heal from the inside out is the key."
—Wynonna Judd, singer and entertainer

CHAPTER 12
REDEFINING NORMAL

"Normal is so overrated."

–Cheri Hamilton in the movie SOUL SURFER

In the movie SOUL SURFER, there is a scene in which Bethany tries on a prosthetic (man-made) arm and sadly realizes that it won't make her look or feel normal. She runs to her room and winds up having a great talk with her mom about what normal means and how much it is really worth.

All of us can feel under pressure to fit in. To dress like other people. To talk like them, look like them, and even behave like them. There's no escaping the fact that we live in a world with lots of other people, and nobody wants to feel like they're not acceptable. But what happens when life changes your definition of normal? Or what do you do if you've been born with a different appearance or a unique challenge? Read on, and you'll meet some fascinating people who will help you realize, "Normal is so overrated!"

And now it is time for fascinatingly "normal" trivia. Did you know ...

It's normal in America to signal someone to come by holding out your index finger and curling it toward you. *In Singapore, this gesture signifies death.*

It is normal in America to be told you must eat everything on your plate before leaving the table. *In the African country of Zimbabwe, cleaning your plate insults your host by implying you didn't really get enough to eat.*

We try hard to be as normal as possible—just blending in, being cool, and not getting noticed for anything out of the ordinary.

It is normal (and safer) to drive on the right side of the road in America. *In England, the rules of the road are to drive on the left side of the road (but the right side of the car).*

Did any of these surprise you? Do you see what these facts reveal? Normal isn't always, well . . . normal. Normal might be what we're used to, but often it's just a perception. It might be part of our culture, but it's more popular opinion than scientific fact. It's usually based on what's common or true for the majority of people, but sometimes our vision is still too small to see the big picture.

It was normal at one time to view the world as flat, but of course that was wrong. It was normal in the eighteenth century for men to wear powdered wigs with long curled hair. That was just plain wrong too, but in more of a you've-got-to-be-kidding way. Bell-bottoms (pants and jeans that get wider from the knee down) were normal in the 1970s but not in the 1980s. Then they became normal again in the 1990s; they were called flare-leg then. But by the early 2000s, skinny jeans took over as normal, and flare-legs faded out again.

The world of fashion calls normal *in, hot,* or *trendsetting,* and it's ever changing. Trying to follow what people say is normal can jerk you around so fast you get whiplash.

Most of us try to keep up with normal because being different can make us feel lonely and inferior. That's no fun. We try hard to be as normal as possible—just blending in, being cool, and not getting noticed for anything out of the ordinary. Maybe you've felt that way if you had to get glasses or if you were the first in your class to wear braces. Maybe you've gotten used to them by now, so they're normal to you. But at first it was probably hard, and you felt like you looked different from everyone else.

Let's talk about an extreme time in history when the idea of what is normal became a matter of life and death. Though it was long before you were born, you probably know about Adolf Hitler and Nazi Germany, right? Hitler, a German political leader turned dictator began telling everyone that the people of the Aryan race, those who had blonde hair and blue eyes, were superior to everyone else. Since this characterized the mainstream of the German people, Hitler declared them normal and all others "not normal." He then argued that since they were superior to everyone else, they should rule the world.

Many liked thinking of themselves as part of a superior race of people. Many others went along with his thinking because they were afraid to speak up. And yes, there were others who did their best to fight against this terrible lie about who was normal and who wasn't.

Because Hitler and his Nazi army felt they had the right, if not the duty, to control countries of "lesser" peoples, they soon attacked their neighbors. It wasn't long until the entire world was caught up in a fight so big it was called a world war.

The horrible lie Hitler told came down especially hard on the Jewish people who lived in Germany and the surrounding areas. Their physical characteristics and heritage made them easy to identify as so-called outsiders. Hitler convinced his followers that Jews were so abnormal, they weren't worth keeping alive. They were rounded up and treated as though they weren't even human beings. Millions were killed simply because they didn't measure up to what Hitler said was normal.

Can you see how this *normal* and *not-normal* business can get messed up?

So how can you tell what's good normal or bad normal? First, ask yourself who you look to for what's normal and what's not. Popular people at school? Actors and rock stars? Reality-television shows? Video game worlds? Your own crowd of friends and family?

WHAT DEFINES NORMAL

When Bethany Hamilton got home from the hospital, she had to start dealing with all the challenges that came from missing an arm. It used to be normal to cut up fruit to make a smoothie. It used to be normal to get dressed and tie her bathing suit. And it used to be normal to look, well, normal, like most people with two arms.

She had to get used to it all, and so did other people. Strangers stared at her or asked questions. How would you feel if everyone around took one look at you and thought, *Not normal*? Bethany tried a prosthetic arm, hoping it would make her look normal again, at least from a distance. But it only felt awkward and didn't help her function any better—she hated it.

There's a powerful scene in the movie *Soul Surfer* where Bethany gets so frustrated, she breaks the arm off a Barbie doll so it will look more like her new idea of normal. She hated being different, wondered what boy would want to date someone with just one arm, and wondered if she'd never be *normal* again. (Maybe you've asked questions like that.) When Bethany was struggling with all those feelings, her mom gave her an awesome nugget of wisdom: "Normal is so overrated."

Hmm, Bethany's mom is on to something. Let's think about it for a few minutes.

Think of the most normal person you know. List some of that person's characteristics.

Now think of someone who inspires you or who's had a big impact on your life. List some of this person's characteristics.

Now compare the two lists. How much are they different and how much are they alike? It's likely that you can see that the people who inspire and impact you probably aren't exactly normal. They rise above the norm somehow and make you think, *Wow, I want to be like that!* Many of them have paddled into God's wave for their lives, soul surfing toward their dreams and becoming who God created them to be.

ABNORMALLY GREAT

When you start to pay attention, you realize that nobody is normal in every area of life. And those people who inspire you have actually made the most of the things that make them different. They're the ones who have sent the concept of normal to outer space and back again. Check out these people who have exceeded the idea of normal.

Bubble Ball raced to more than seven million downloads to become the number one free game app downloaded from the Apple iTunes store. It knocked off Angry Birds, an app that had been king for a year. No big deal? It is when you realize Bubble Ball was designed and created by a fourteen-year-old!

Robert Nay is good with computers. All his friends knew it, so one said, "Hey, Robert, why don't you make an app?" *Why not?* thought Robert. So he went to the public library in Spanish Fork, Utah, where he lives, and started learning how. There were times the teen questioned if he could really pull it off, but he just kept trying until he did it.

Robert was designing his next app when this book was published, but he was keeping it a secret. Oh, and he planned to charge at least a buck a download next time. A dollar a download for Bubble Ball would have topped seven million dollars. Not exactly normal pay for a part-time job!

On the other end of the age spectrum is a college student—but as you might guess by now—a far-from-normal college student. Nola Ochs was ninety-five when she graduated from Fort Hays State University in 2007! She was ninety-eight when she earned her master's degree from the same school. Most ninety-eight-year-olds are fortunate to be playing checkers at the old folks home, not graduating from college.

Nola actually thought her life was about over when her husband died back in 1972. Instead, she started taking college classes a few years later. She chose classes that sounded interesting and realized she loved learning. Nola had attended college before—way back in 1930. She earned a teacher's certificate and taught in country schools in Kansas. Then she got married, raised four sons, and worked on the family farm.

When Nola graduated from Fort Hays State, she was about seventy-five years older than most of her classmates. Her plans after graduation included teaching at the college and taking more classes for fun.

Then there's Ana Dodson. Her life looked pretty normal as she grew up in Colorado. But Ana wanted to understand where she came from. See, unlike her friends in Colorado, Ana was born in Peru. She was four weeks old when she was adopted by the Dodsons. As she got older, Ana had a lot of questions about her birthplace. So the Dodsons took Ana back to Peru for a visit when she was eleven.

Ana took teddy bears and books to give to the kids she knew she'd meet there, but she quickly realized that their needs went much deeper. In response, Ana started Peruvian Hearts. The nonprofit organization brings education, nutrition, and health care to many kids who live in extreme poverty. Ana's organization has raised more than forty thousand dollars, providing hope and opportunities for hundreds of kids.

EMBRACE YOUR ABNORMALITY

So you're inspired by these people, but what is it that's "not normal" about you? Do you feel your own not-so-normal characteristics aren't cool enough or great enough to pursue? Maybe you feel like they just make you strange. That brings us back to the primary question in this chapter: who decides what's normal in your life?

It might help you to answer this if you can remember what we talked about at the very beginning of this book. You weren't created normal. You are God's intricate and unique design. He has given you special gifts with the potential to launch you way beyond normal. That dream in your heart? Normal can't contain it. The new things you've learned on your path to healing? Normal can't touch that. God invites you to much more than normal. He wants you to learn from Him what's His best and most wonderful normal for you.

God's normal for you begins with putting your trust in Jesus and accepting deep down inside you that you are God's child and Jesus' friend

When Jesus lived on earth, He totally changed what people thought was normal. He took all the old rules and showed them how God intended for them to be lived out. That's why so many people were drawn to Him and believed in Him. They wanted to let God decide what was normal. But it's also why other people, especially the religious leaders of the day, didn't like Him. They liked *their* version of normal. It gave them a sense of power, and they thought they had God all figured out. The problem was that they weren't willing to really trust Him. The normal that Jesus brought turned everything upside down—in the very best possible way.

Being a soul surfer means looking into your own soul and remembering who God created you to be.

So whose idea of normal do you accept when it comes to beauty, strength, attitude, outlook, or social status? You can never go wrong when you listen and look to God, the ultimate soul surfer. Being a soul surfer means looking into your own soul and remembering who God created you to be.

How do you do that? It starts with giving Him your life, believing that He's God, and asking Him to forgive all the wrong you've done. Then you keep it going by following Him every day.

Have you ever used a compass? It always points north. It's magnetized so its normal is north. And by looking at it, you can tell which way you're headed and keep on the right path. It's a guide. If you've ever been a Girl Scout or Boy Scout, you know about that.

Agreeing with what God says is your normal is like using His compass. When you read the Bible, pray, and worship Him, you are checking His compass. It keeps you heading in God's direction, and it tunes you into God's north—His normal. The more you do it, the more it becomes part of you, and the more like Jesus you become. The more God-normal you become, the more you'll see how you stand out beyond the world's view of normal, in the best possible ways.

YOUR RIDE

Make a list of some areas in your life that you would like to be abnormally great in. Write a description of what that might look like.

"Once you live a good story, you get a taste for a kind of meaning in life, and you can't go back to being normal."
—Donald Miller, author and public speaker

"To be normal is the ideal aim of the unsuccessful."
—Carl Gustav Jung, Swiss psychiatrist and founder of analytic psychology

"Refuse to be average. Let your heart soar as high as it will."
—A. W. Tozer, pastor and author

"The only normal people are the ones you don't know very well."
—Alfred Adler, Austrian psychologist

CHAPTER 13
FAMILY AND FRIENDS

"Bethany, grab my leash.
I'll pull you the rest of the way out."

–Alana Blanchard to Bethany Hamilton in the movie SOUL SURFER

In the movie SOUL SURFER, Bethany has a tough time in the first surfing competition she enters after losing her arm. She gets caught in the impact zone and can't get out past the big waves. But even in rough water, what Bethany definitely has is a great family and loyal friends. As her friends and family cheer for her on the shore, Bethany's BFF Alana paddles over to try to help. Alana even knocks Bethany's rival Malina off her surfboard to get back at her for what she'd done to her friend.

When you're struggling and in pain, you want to look for support from your family and your friends. Even if they're not perfect, they can still have your back. In this chapter, we're going to talk about how to build strong relationships with the people closest to you. And how you can become a great tow-in partner for someone else!

There are surfers, and then there are big-wave surfers. Most surfers will do anything to get in the waves, but only a select few want to tangle with the ocean when the waves start reaching the size of skyscrapers—walls of water fifty-, sixty-, eighty-feet high, or more. Do you know how tall that is? It's a five-, six-, or eight-story building! Imagine riding *that* while it's trying to fall on you.

Those are the *tow-in* surfers. It's called tow-in because *these* surfers get towed behind a Jet Ski on their boards while they hold on to a water ski rope. Once they get going fast enough, they slingshot onto monster waves. These waves are so gigantic and so fast that being pulled behind a Jet Ski is the only way a surfer can get enough momentum to catch and ride them.

Obviously, you have to have two people to tow-in surf: one to drive the Jet Ski and one to surf. You also have to have two people to survive. See, the Jet Ski driver is also the rescue driver. Remember how we talked about the impact zone and how bad it can be to get drilled by wave after wave? Multiply that by a hundred in these mammoth waves. Tow-in surfers wear flotation vests to help them get back to the surface if they fall, but getting stuck in the impact zone with a wave this size can be particularly deadly. There's so much water that surfers are pushed deep under the surface.

For this type of surfing, a good tow-in partner is a lifesaver. The Jet Ski driver pulls the surfer onto a rescue sled behind the ski. Then together they gun it for safety as fast as they can. Is it any surprise that tow-in partners are good buddies? They put their lives in each other's hands. Tow-in surfers must have complete trust that their partners will be there to save them when they need it.

The same thing is true in the life of a soul surfer. We all need other people, especially when things go wrong and we're surfacing after a really bad day or problem. We don't necessarily need a friend with a Jet Ski, although that could make for a fun ride. Instead, our family and friends are our lifelines. They're the ones who know us best. They're the ones who tell us when to go for it and when to hold back. Their encouragement gives us strength, and they are the ones who stay close by to rescue us when life explodes around us.

Whisper a word of thanks to God for the family and friends He's placed in your life. Even the Bible talks about how important they are: *"A friend loves at all times, and a brother [or sister] is born for adversity"* (Proverbs 17:17). Lean on them. Don't try to go it alone.

TRUE FRIENDS

Tori Davies and three of her friends were on a backpacking trip together when the weather turned bad. The British sixteen-year-olds were prepared, but the conditions got bad quick. When they reached the river they had to cross, it was raging from all the hail and rain runoff.

Tori went first and made the crossing safely, but Susannah Burtinshaw got her foot stuck in a hole and slipped. She sprained her ankle but managed to grab a rock. The current was strong and rushed around her. She could barely hold on. That's when Tori and the others leaped into action. They knew they needed to get Susannah's heavy pack off before it pulled their friend down into the water and swept her away.

Tori shouted instructions and waded back into the waters. She found shelter in an eddy (water that flows in the opposite direction of the normal flow of the river) behind a big rock and was able to reach Susannah and pull her to safety. Hypothermia was still a risk, though, for the cold, wet girls. But Tori set up an emergency shelter that she had brought along—even though her friends had laughed at her for carrying it when they started out. The girls were able to warm themselves and call for help. Then, they sang songs while they waited for the mountain rescue team to come. Happily, they all made it home safely.

It's a good thing Susannah had a friend like Tori when she needed help. Tori was prepared and ready to do whatever she could for her friend. And she stayed calm in Susannah's crisis.

You might never need a friend to literally save your life, but then again, you might. And even if the dangers and problems aren't physical, there are plenty of daily problems that could threaten to sweep you away.

In those kinds of situations, who would you trust with your life? Think about it for a minute. That person should be someone who ...

- knows you really well—your past, present, and dreams for the future.
- knows and respects your strengths and talents.
- loves you.
- knows your weaknesses and faults.
- still loves you.
- is committed to you for the long haul.
- is positive, encouraging, and wise.
- is part of your everyday life.
- makes you laugh.
- can talk or just hang out with you in silence.

- knows your values and beliefs and respects them.

Write down the names of the people in your life who best match these characteristics. If you've got a long list, narrow it down. Casual friendships are fine—you need those too. But we're talking about the truest BFFs—the ones you can trust with your life, who have your back, who will never let you down (or at least hardly ever; everybody is human)—the few deepest friendships. Who's a true match for that? It's probably a short list.

If you came up blank, it's time to reach out to people who care and take some steps to find those supportive people God intends for your life. Without them, you're asking to go down in the impact zone. Start with your parents and maybe even a brother or sister. Try a youth leader at church or a teacher; you might not hang out with them, but you know you can trust them with the big stuff. They can even give good advice about finding some friends your own age. And keep reading—the next part of this chapter has tips for making friends.

Before we go there, is your boyfriend or girlfriend one of the people on your list? That's fine. But is he or she the only person on your list? That's not so good. Don't fall into the trap of putting all your eggs in the romance basket. A boyfriend or girlfriend might stand by you, but romantic relationships can change fast and get complicated, especially when the going gets tough. Make sure you're spending time with your other friends and putting energy into those friendships, as well.

BE A FRIEND

You may already be blessed with good friends. If not, you may be wondering how to connect with others in a meaningful way or what the best way is to be a true friend to others. No matter what's going on in your life, there's someone who needs you. Take this quiz and see how you score on the true-friend scale:

1. You notice there's a new kid in your class. You …

a. pretend you don't notice. Maybe he'll go away.

b. give her a glance and a half-smile but don't say anything.

c. introduce yourself and invite her to eat lunch with you and your friends.

2. You had a fight with your best friend. You …

a. give her the silent treatment for a week.

b. pretend it never happened but eventually start hanging out again.

c. apologize for your part of the wrong.

3. Your friend has a big musical performance. You ...

a. totally forget.

b. go but miss his part because you stay in the lobby talking the whole time.

c. go early so you can give her a good-luck card you made.

4. A group of your friends starts laughing and making fun of an unpopular girl. You ...

a. laugh and join in.

b. don't laugh and don't say anything.

c. tell your friends to stop and ask how they'd feel if they were the brunt of jokes like that.

5. Your friend is having a really bad day. You ...

a. laugh at her.

b. hope things get better, but there's nothing you can really do, right?

c. buy him a snack and tell him you're there if he wants to talk.

6. You go someplace where you don't know anyone. You ...

a. hang in the back and don't say a word.

b. say hi when a couple people say hi to you.

c. look for someone standing alone and introduce yourself.

7. You're talking with a friend. You ...

a. keep interrupting her stories to tell what happened to *you*.

b. listen but avoid talking about what's on your mind.

c. listen closely, ask lots of questions, and answer her questions honestly about what's going on with you.

How'd you do? Give yourself 0 points for every *a* answer, 1 point for every *b* and 3 points for each *c*. Add them up and see how you did.

0-6 points: You need some work on your friendship skills. Your actions say you care only about yourself, and that will drive friends away—if that hasn't happened already.

7-14 points: Your conscience is guiding a good friend-sense, but you need some courage to put your good instincts into action. God can help you with that by giving you courage. All you have to do is ask.

15-21 points: Your friendship shows through as true because you pay attention to other people's needs. Keep it up, and you'll find you have many true friends in return.

THE FAMILY FACTOR

Your kidneys are really important. They regulate blood pressure and supply in your body and remove body waste. Most people have two kidneys, but you can live with only one. And there are almost ninety thousand people in the United States who need kidney transplants right now to give them one working organ. Some of those sick people wait because they can't find a matching kidney that their body will accept, and some wait because there aren't enough kidneys available.

Jake Orta from California was eleven when he got his first transplant. He didn't have to wait long. His dad was eager to sacrifice a kidney to save his son's life, and he was a perfect match for donation. The operation went well, but an infection six months later weakened Jake's new kidney, and it eventually failed a few years later. Jake needed another kidney.

No problem, thought Jake's identical twin, Johnny. *I'll give him one of mine.* It seemed to make perfect sense, but it was against the medical rules that said only adults could donate organs. Finally, the doctors agreed it was okay and successfully moved a kidney from one seventeen-year-old brother to the other.

It was a gift of life for Jake. It was not a difficult decision for Johnny. Both of the brothers had a long recovery. They both missed much of their junior year of high school, including prom. But they healed well and got back to deejaying together and living normal lives.

Jake and Johnny no doubt have their fights and disagreements. But no matter what happens, they know that they are there for each other and for the other members of their family. Both of them are willing to give whatever it takes.

Like 'em, love 'em, or totally can't stand 'em, there's nobody else in the world like your family. They're who you come from and who shape you. Your family members have known you longer than anyone else. They see you at your best and your worst. They share your history, not to mention your genetic code. And they're most likely going to be there in your future. Your family might be solid as a rock, or they might put the fun in dys*fun*ctional. Either way, there are probably times when they drive you crazy and other times when they inspire you.

Your parents and brothers and sisters can be your greatest tow-in partners when life is throwing you some big waves.

No matter how things are with your family, don't give up on them. Reach out to them. Unless there's real abuse or neglect going on in your family, we encourage you to value and pursue those relationships. It might not be easy! It may mean facing hard stuff, getting past hurt feelings, and forgiving anger and personality differences, but the payoffs are worth it. Your parents and brothers and sisters can be your greatest tow-in partners when life is throwing you some big waves.

But you don't understand! You don't know my family! It's true that we don't know the specific details of your family and life. But we do know that your relationships might feel more strained now than when you were a little kid. That's natural. You're growing toward being your own independent person as you become a young adult. You probably feel like you're ready to be there now. In some ways you are, but in some ways you aren't. Remember that big-picture, whole-process thing we've talked about?

That's the way growing up is too. Your parents want you to get there: grown up, independent, and mature. But they can often see how the process is going even when you can't. They might make mistakes in their relationships with you, but remember that they love you and want the very best for you even when you feel like they're terrible ogres trying to spoil your fun. Show them some grace, and you'll probably find that they'll do the same. As you reach out to build the bridges with your family, you can find some of the strongest support around.

THE FAMILY OF GOD

Also, be sure you don't forget about the strength and support that comes from another kind of family—the family of God. When you make the choice to place your heart in God's hands, He adopts you as His very own child. That's why we call Him our heavenly Father. You become part of His family, and all the other people who have become His children are your brothers and sisters. That family bond runs deep.

Those brothers and sisters in faith can pray for you and remind you of God's love and His plans for your life. They can sympathize with your challenges and remind you that God is riding those waves with you, ready to pull you up out of the thrashing waters of the impact zone into the God zone. The Bible even tells us that's what God wants us to do for each other. It says, *"Therefore encourage one another and build each other up"* (1 Thessalonians 5:11).

Lean on other people around you who are soul surfing with God. And most of all, reach out to God, the One who knows and loves you with the perfect love that even other humans can't give you. Talk to Him and ask Him for what you need. He is always listening.

That's what Ryan Hall found out in middle school. Ryan is now one of the best marathon runners in the country. He qualified for the 2008 Beijing Olympics by wiping out the US Olympic trials record, but back then he was just discovering his passion for running and the dream God gave him. When Ryan got serious about running, though, he stopped playing other sports, and slowly his friends drifted away. Nobody else ran. Nobody shared Ryan's passion. And then many of his friends started getting into partying and making bad choices. Ryan felt lonely, but he knew Jesus was there for him. Ryan responded by making Jesus his best friend. He talked to Him and spent time reading the Bible. Ryan ran and worshipped God. Eventually, he made more friends, and running led him to his wife when he was in college. Ryan has never forgotten that his best friend, Jesus, never once let him down.

Reach out to God, the One who knows and loves you with the perfect love that even other humans can't give you.

A WEB OF LOVE

You know how spiderwebs work: They have superthin but superstrong fiber. A spider can use a single strand to move around some, but that one line isn't enough to keep it alive. It needs to connect that string to many different points and intertwine it together to catch food and get nourishment. And when strong winds blow, the web draws support from every side and holds together.

You're like that spider. You need a strong web that's connected to other people. You can get around a little by yourself, but when the winds of hard times pick up, you need the support of others. Another way to picture it is that you have an invisible ball of string with one end tied to you. You need to pass it to your closest friends and family so they can grab on to it too. Each day you might be tempted not to pass the ball of string or to throw it as far away as you can, but you need to pass that string to others by sharing your frustrations and hopes, forgiving each other, and working together. Passing the ball of string around builds a steady web of support that can nourish you and keep you strong.

YOUR RIDE

Look at your list of the people you trust your life with. Text them and let them know how much you appreciate them. If you came up blank on good friends, list three people you'd like to connect with. Invite them to do something fun and get started toward a friendship you can count on through the storms of life.

"The only way to have a friend is to be one."
—Ralph Waldo Emerson, American poet

"You don't choose your family. They are God's gift to you, as you are to them."
—Bishop Desmond Tutu, African spiritual leader and novelist

"Nothing but heaven itself is better than a friend who is really a friend."
—Titus Maccius Plautus, Roman playwright

"The greatest healing therapy is friendship and love."
—Hubert H. Humphrey, former US vice president

PART 5

Back in the Water

CATCHING GOD'S WAVE

Isaiah 41:10

Do not fear, for I am with you; do not be dismayed, for I am your God. I will strengthen you and help you; I will uphold you with my righteous right hand.

1 Corinthians 16:13

Be on your guard; stand firm in the faith; be men of courage; be strong.

Romans 12:21

Do not be overcome by evil, but overcome evil with good.

1 John 5:5

Who is it that overcomes the world? Only he who believes that Jesus is the Son of God.

2 Chronicles 15:7

Be strong and do not give up, for your work will be rewarded.

1 Corinthians 15:57

Thanks be to God! He gives us the victory through our Lord Jesus Christ.

CHAPTER 14

DEALING WITH THE
F-WORD: FEAR

"Aren't you afraid?"
"I'm more afraid of not surfing."

–Alana Blanchard and Bethany Hamilton in the movie SOUL SURFER

In the movie SOUL SURFER, *Bethany comes to the point where she has to decide whether she's going to get back in the water and try to surf again. For most people, getting into the ocean doesn't seem too frightening. But Bethany and Alana didn't just know there were sharks in the water* somewhere; *they had actually seen a huge one come up out of the waves and attack Bethany. Both of them had memories of that terrible morning.*

Fear is a natural part of life, and a healthy fear of unsafe situations and even scary critters like sharks, snakes, and hairy brown wolf spiders can keep us safe. But there are times when all of us have to confront what we're afraid of and then keep on going. Read on, and you'll hear about some people who did exactly that!

People are scared of all kinds of things. There are phobias of almost everything you can imagine—and then some. You name it, and somebody's probably afraid of it. Just for fun, see if you can match the phobia on the left with its meaning on the right. (Answers at the end of this chapter.)

AGRIZOOPHOBIA	Fear of waves
ARACHIBUTYROPHOBIA	Fear of stars
BLENNOPHOBIA	Fear of wild animals
CHRONOMENTROPHOBIA	Fear of belly buttons
EPHEBIPHOBIA	Fear of peanut butter sticking to the roof of the mouth
KYMOPHOBIA	Fear of teenagers
LACHANOPHOBIA	Fear of telephones
OMPHALOPHOBIA	Fear of vegetables
SIDEROPHOBIA	Fear of slime
TELEPHONOPHOBIA	Fear of clocks

Crazy, isn't it? It's actually funny to think about all the things we can be afraid of. Former president Franklin D. Roosevelt said, "The only thing we have to fear is fear itself." That's very inspiring, but realistically, we all feel afraid sometimes.

So what is fear anyway?

Fear is an emotion that is often triggered when we face danger or feel pain. It gives us a jolt, and our brains decide in milliseconds whether to run away or stand and fight.

That kind of fear is natural. It is part of our physical makeup to help us survive. If we aren't careful, though, fear can take control of our lives, shutting us down emotionally and keeping us from pursuing our dreams. God tells us in the Bible that we aren't to let fear have the upper hand. When fear starts getting pushy and possessive rather than simply alerting us to danger, we must tackle it and defeat it with faith and trust in our loving and powerful heavenly Father. In Isaiah 41:10 we find this verse: *"Don't panic. I'm with you. There's no need to fear for I'm your God. I'll give you strength. I'll help you. I'll hold you steady, keep a firm grip on you"* (MSG).

> **"Courage is doing what you're afraid to do. There can be no courage unless you're scared."**
>
> -Eddie Rickenbacker

FULL SPEED AHEAD

Waking up to find out your apartment building is on fire is always scary. That's what happened to Alex Jeffrey, a seventeen-year-old student in Edinburgh, Scotland. The thick smoke woke her up, and Alex realized she was trapped in the top-floor apartment by the flames below. She called for help from the bedroom window, and firefighters raised a tall ladder to rescue her.

But another problem surfaced. Alex had an intense fear of heights. Now she was faced with what seemed like an impossible choice: stay in a burning building or climb out a window onto a skinny ledge and dangle from a ladder several stories off the ground. Alex made the right choice. She pushed back her fear, chose the ladder, and was safely rescued. Alex's experience reveals an important point about fear: Sometimes to beat fear, you've got to go straight through it.

But the choice isn't always as clear as it was in Alex's situation—burning building or high ladder.

Bethany Hamilton had to make a choice about going back in the water after being attacked by a shark. In the movie *Soul Surfer,* her friend Alana asked, "Aren't you afraid?" as they headed into the water. Bethany answered, "I'm more afraid of not surfing." There was some fear on either side of the choice, but Bethany wouldn't let fear stop her. She could see her dream on the other side of the fear. She focused on the dream God had placed in her heart, and she plunged in.

You can handle the fears in your life the same way by looking past them. Maybe you are fearful of speaking in front of a group, but you know the dream God has given you is to carry a message of hope to others. You could do that one person at a time, but think how many more people you could reach by talking to groups of people. So you make a choice to dismiss the fear, place yourself in God's hands, and push through. Faith, hope, and action are three of God's best weapons against fear.

It's time to take the first step toward facing your fears—identifying what they are.

What scares you?

_____

_____

_____

How could each of those fears affect your dream?

_____

_____

_____

What steps can you take to conquer your fears? (Don't forget about the God zone.)

_____

_____

_____

Tackling your real-life fears head on can provide another benefit, as well. When you get through it to the other side, you often find yourself saying, "Hey, that wasn't so bad. I didn't really have so much to be afraid of after all."

THE GOD FACTOR

So do you think fear ever goes away? You know all those heroic people in stories, movies, legends, and the Bible who accomplish great things and achieve their dreams? Do you think they all reached a place where they just weren't afraid anymore? It's not likely.

Fear is always lurking, looking for a place to put down roots and cause trouble. Even when you've faced it head on and won, you must remain watchful. It's likely that you will have to conquer fear many times—maybe even every time you take a positive step toward your dream. You may never feel completely comfortable speaking in front of a group. You will have to choose to push it aside every single time you stand up to speak. But you can do it with God's help. He will always, without exception, be there to back you up and help you get through it. It probably won't be just one big victory but rather many victories that will ensure you reach your dream. Each time, you will have to make a choice, trust God, and be courageous.

The Bible tells us of a man named Joshua. He had a gigantic dream and a very challenging God-job. He was to move a whole nation of people on foot from one place to another. Along the way, Joshua and the people God had entrusted him with would face great danger and daunting obstacles. Joshua 1:9 records what God said to Joshua about what they were facing. He didn't try to minimize the dangers and hardships ahead, but said, *"This is my command—be strong and courageous! Do not be afraid or discouraged. For the LORD your God is with you wherever you go"* (NLT).

WHAT IS COURAGE?

"Courage is doing what you're afraid to do. There can be no courage unless you're scared." A guy named Eddie Rickenbacker said that, and he would know. He is considered to be the best American fighter pilot in World War I. Have you ever played one of those air-battle video games where the goal is to shoot enemy planes out of the air while avoiding being shot down yourself? Well, Captain Rickenbacker did that in real life. And he was über good at it! So good that he was called the Ace of Aces.

Day after day, Captain Rickenbacker flew out to face the Red Baron and other seriously dangerous pilots belonging to an infamous group called the Flying Circus. In those days, biplanes were used. The pilots' heads stuck out of the tops of their planes, so they wore goggles to protect their eyes and scarves around their necks. They could see the enemy shooting straight at them with nothing to block the bullets—just imagine!

But Captain Rickenbacker had a way of surviving crazy-bad situations. The news twice reported that he had been killed.

The first time was when he was in a commercial airliner crash in 1941. His body was broken all over; he was pinned in the wreckage and covered with gas for nine hours before he was rescued. It was a miracle that he lived, and even more so when you consider that he instructed and encouraged the other survivors during his ordeal. Captain Rickenbacker faced death again during World War II. He was no longer in the military, but the head of the US Air Force sent him on a special mission to inspect some bases in the Pacific Ocean. The old bomber he was riding in had to crash land in the water, way off course. Captain Rickenbacker and seven other passengers made it out of the plane, into rubber life rafts, and they floated lost and undiscovered at sea for twenty-two days! The only food they started out with was four oranges. Captain Rickenbacker gave the men orders and kept all but one of them alive. Do you think Captain Rickenbacker was scared in all those situations? Of course he was. But he accomplished great things because he never let fear stop him.

Fourteen-year old Cora Lindberg from San Diego, California, was terrified when she heard an explosion and saw her dad on fire in the driveway. He had been repairing an engine when he was splattered with gas that then ignited. "Stop, drop, and roll!" she yelled. "Stop, drop, and roll!" Her father did that, but the flames kept burning. Cora ran for a hose and sprayed water all over her father, saving his life. Doctors said he probably would have died if the fire had blazed only a few seconds longer.

Cora could have been paralyzed by fear. Imagine yourself in her shoes. It must have been terrifying. But she didn't let her fear win. She reacted quickly and did what had to be done.

What about you? With every frightening situation, you have a choice. Let fear take over or act courageously. You may not face war in the skies, but you most likely face real deadly enemies every day, like drugs, alcohol, and sexual temptations. You might not be confronted with actual flames, but every day you face invisible flames that lick at you with doubts about whether you're good enough, attractive enough, popular enough, or smart enough. You need courage to face all of these enemies.

We don't know where Captain Rickenbacker and Cora Lindberg got their courage. But we do know where you can get yours. The Bible says,

"God has not given us a spirit of fear and timidity, but of power, love, and self-discipline" (2 Timothy 1:7, NLT). To those who follow Him, God gives His supernatural courage. With it, you can stomp on fear whenever and wherever you find it.

FEAR AND ANXIETY

So far we've talked about fear that is sudden and unexpected. But there is another type of fear that many people, maybe even you, may find difficult to deal with. It's kind of a general, overall fear and anxiety, not about what *is* happening but about what *could* happen. You may feel like you are never outside its grip. It can keep you stuck, unable to move forward into what God has planned for you.

If you suffer from this type of fear, you should talk to your parents or some other trusted adult in your life. You might need to see a doctor. Sometimes, there are physical reasons why people suffer with this type of generalized fear and anxiety. There are medications that can help.

Prayer is also important. You can pray with confidence, knowing with certainty that God did not place this in your life. He wants you to be free. In 1 Peter 5:7 we read: *"Cast all your anxiety on him because he cares for you."*

One more weapon against fear and anxiety is reading the Bible—God's Word. Jesus said, *"You will know the truth, and the truth will set you free"* (John 8:32). So find specific verses in the Bible on overcoming fear and anxiety. Then write them down on an index card or notepad so you will be able to refer to them throughout the day. You might even want to memorize them

Overcoming fear takes strength and courage, but you don't have to go it alone.

and say them out loud to yourself often. This will build faith into your life and remind you how much God loves you.

DO NOT FEAR

Like other obstacles you may encounter in life, fear is easier to overcome with the support of friends and family. They can't overcome your fear for you, but their encouragement can make a big difference. They can also help you decide when it's a good idea or just plain stupid to dive headlong into something with a no-fear attitude.

Yes, overcoming fear takes strength and courage, but you don't have to go it alone. Family, friends, and especially God are there to help. That can make all the difference. It's easier to make the right choices when you are certain you are loved and supported.

Like we talked about in the beginning of this chapter, fear keeps us away from danger. But God wants to teach us how to keep fear in its place so that we can go about the business of capturing our dreams and becoming everything He intends us to be.

He is always there no matter what you are facing. He is reaching out His arms to you, loving you, eager to care for you. He is there to pick you up when you fall and carry you when you can't carry yourself. He loves you more than you will ever know. Keep your focus on Him and let Him help you push right on through whatever fears you may encounter.

PHOBIA ANSWERS

AGRIZOOPHOBIA—Fear of wild animals

ARACHIBUTYROPHOBIA—Fear of peanut butter sticking to the roof of the mouth

BLENNOPHOBIA—Fear of slime

CHRONOMENTROPHOBIA—Fear of clocks

EPHEBIPHOBIA—Fear of teenagers

KYMOPHOBIA—Fear of waves

LACHANOPHOBIA—Fear of vegetables

OMPHALOPHOBIA—Fear of belly buttons

SIDEROPHOBIA—Fear of stars

TELEPHONOPHOBIA—Fear of telephones

YOUR RIDE

Wash your fears away. Find a stick of chalk and use it to write your fears on the sidewalk or patio. Now get out the hose. The water represents your courage, your God-strength, and your power to move past fear. Spray your list of fears and watch them disappear.

"Courage is doing what you're afraid to do. There can be no courage unless you're scared."
—Captain Eddie Rickenbacker, former US fighter pilot

"Courage does not always roar. Sometimes courage is the little voice at the end of the day that says I'll try again tomorrow."
—Mary Anne Radmacher, writer and artist

"Man cannot discover new oceans unless he has the courage to lose sight of the shore."
—André Gide, French writer and Nobel Prize winner

"Courage is fear that has said its prayers."
—Dorothy Bernard, silent movie actress

CHAPTER 15

OVERCOMING WHAT STOPS YOU

"I think I wanna compete. ... We need to figure out something. Some way so when I duck dive, I don't get pounded."

–Bethany Hamilton to her dad in the movie SOUL SURFER

In the movie SOUL SURFER, one of the challenges Bethany faces is how she is going to make it through big waves with only one arm. She can no longer use both arms to push her surfboard down and "duck dive" under the waves. In the movie, Bethany goes to her dad and asks him to help her figure a way around the problem. And being the cool dad that he is, Tom Hamilton has already built a special board for Bethany.

Have you ever been cruising along in life and run into an obstacle? Something that stops you in your tracks and makes you, as a GPS would say, "calculate a new route"? In this chapter, we're going to talk about overcoming the obstacles that sometimes fall into our path.

So you're walking down the road on a beautiful sunny day. Birds are singing and landing on your shoulder. The ice cream truck is giving away free cones and frozen treats. Dogs are frolicking in the grass and cats are sleeping in the sun. Your favorite song is playing out of nowhere. And there's an announcement from the sky that school is now closed—for the rest of the year! It's a perfect day.

You're practically skipping along until you come to an extra large stop sign that's bright and flashing. Okay, so you stop, glance both ways, and then keep groovin' on. No big deal.

The music out of nowhere keeps playing and shuffling all your favorite songs. People are waving. In fact, you're waving to a friend when you almost bump into a great big orange detour sign pointing you another way. Okay, so you take a turn, then another, and yet another as you follow the detour path. It seems a little out of your way, but eventually the detour leads you back to your road, and you keep cruising.

You're just wondering how anybody's ever going to believe that you sang a duet with a songbird who whistled along in harmony like something out of a cartoon when   whoa! Another sign? This time it's actually a great big "Road Closed" with barricades and flashing lights. What is up with all these signs? But you're determined to go on, and you can't see any problem up ahead. So you step around the sign, climb over a few concrete walls, and you're back on your way.

Things seem normal for a little while—until you reach the river. There the road just disappears. The bridge is out, gone, ended. It looks like it just blew up or collapsed. It used to be there. You can see where the road heads up to the water, but then it just disappears. You could keep going—if you want to walk off the edge and drop two hundred feet into the water below. Not a good idea. This looks like the end of the road.

Have you put it together yet? The road we're talking about and the road you're walking on is the road of life. Every day as you follow the path, you come up against all kinds of things that can delay, detour, and even stop you in your tracks. If you plan to keep moving forward, you will have to figure out how to overcome them.

Sometimes, those obstacles come from inside you, like insecurity or fear. But other times, they come from outside you and are beyond your control, like bad weather or too little money. Sometimes, they are real, like a bad grade. And sometimes, they're things you only think are real, like a teacher

It will take wisdom, creativity, faith, and persistence to overcome the obstacles and challenges that will come your way in life.

you think hates you but who really is just challenging you to do your best.

With Him, obstacles are opportunities.

It will take wisdom, creativity, faith, and persistence to overcome the obstacles and challenges that will come your way in life. That's why it's so important to have the strength and wisdom only God can provide. He gives us hope, strength, and wisdom to keep going. He can build a bridge where the bridge is out. He can open the road where it's closed. The way over, through, or around the obstacles might get tough, but you can be tougher. With His help, you can make it!

Look at these scenarios to see how it might all work in real life.

Situation: It's Friday night, and your big school project is due Monday morning. You've known about it for two weeks, but there have been too many other things taking up your time. You know, texts and phone calls from friends, new music to download, team practices, your best friend's latest crisis. It's been crazy. You know you have to get down to business, but it all seems overwhelming now. Only two days to get it done. And after a busy week, you'd rather spend Friday night hanging out with friends, especially when there's a birthday sleepover going on.

Overcome what? Procrastination.

Situation: You just found out your school choir was chosen to sing at the White House. Wow! What an amazing opportunity, but everyone has to pay their own way to Washington, D.C. You worked hard last summer, but you spent that money on a church ski trip. So how are you going to pay for this?

Overcome what? A lack of money.

Situation: You and your best friend are all signed up to go to summer camp together. You've been waiting for years to reach the senior camp, and finally you've made it. You've talked all year about what cute boys will be there, and you know it will pump up your faith in God too. It's going to be so awesome. But it's been a hard year for the camp financially. You get a letter one day that drops a bomb. Your camp is cancelled. The camp itself had to shut down. This can't be happening! Can it?

Overcome what? Disappointment.

TAKE A FEW STEPS

As you can see, an obstacle can come in all shapes and sizes. But no matter what kind it is, if it is getting in the way of what you feel God wants you to do, you have to deal with it. Sound's impossible? It's not, especially since God is there to help. Remember: He's working for your good, and He wants to help you fulfill the dreams He's given you. With Him, obstacles are opportunities.

The Bible tells us, *"If you falter in times of trouble, how small is your strength!"* (Proverbs 24:10). That's pretty clear, isn't it. You don't have to give up, and you don't have to be helpless. In fact, beating the challenges that get in your way can be as easy as 1-2-3.

1. Identify It

Think about your situation. What's the main problem? What's the real obstacle that you need to overcome? The list of possibilities is endless, but here are some common ones.

Temptation	Too much time
Fear	Too little time
Pain	Anger
Laziness	Sadness
Bad weather	Addiction
Wrong location	Procrastination
Lack of skill	Add some of your own challenges:
Lack of money	_____
Lack of opportunity	_____

2. Learn About It

You can't use the same tactic for overcoming every obstacle. Have you ever played on a sports team? Your coach probably didn't suggest using the same strategy for every opponent. Ever heard the phrase "Know your enemy"? When you know your opponent's strengths and weaknesses, you can better figure out how to beat them.

It's the same with the problem that's in your way. The better you understand it—where it came from, how big a deal it really is, who else it affects, and what defeats it—the better you will be at overcoming it. This can be tricky to learn sometimes, especially in the middle of a problem. Be sure to also rely on your friends and family for help. God has put them in your life for times like these, to give you advice, support, and a helping hand.

3. Take It On

Obstacles that aren't overcome start to look a lot like excuses. What's stopping you from pursuing your dream? Are you fighting to get past the roadblocks or giving in to them? Don't make excuses. Instead, commit them to God, ask for His help and guidance, work to overcome them, and watch Him carry you up, over, or around whatever it is that stands in your way.

THE DIFFERENT FACES OF OVERCOMING

If obstacles can look different, overcoming them can too. Need some real-life examples? Here you go.

Overcoming Is Conquering

Mount Rainier is a massive volcano in Washington that rises 14,411 feet above sea level. Each year, about ten thousand people attempt to climb Mount Rainier, and only half make it. Most of those people can see. It's nearly impossible if you're blind.

Captain Scotty Smiley grew up near Mount Rainier, so as he sat at the summit after a grueling climb, he had a clear image of the mountain in his mind. He could see himself sitting on top of that snow-white peak, but Scotty couldn't actually see any of it with his eyes.

That's because the last thing he saw was a car bomber in Iraq just before it exploded near him. Scotty lost one eye, and the other was blinded. Two years later, Scotty's climb up Mount Rainier was painstakingly slow. His guides helped him up rocky trails, across snow fields, and over icy crevasses that dropped into seemingly endless abysses. At one point, Scotty slipped and fell over a cliff, but the rope attached to his climbing team caught and saved him. Scotty never gave up. He kept putting one foot in front of the other, he relied on his team to guide him along the way, and he conquered not only the mountain but his disability, as well.

Sometimes, overcoming the obstacles in our lives means asking for God's help, listening for His wisdom, and then fighting against them with all the strength He gives us. This style of conquering means that no matter what problem blocks our way, we keep going until we beat it.

You know what's awesome? God wants to help you conquer your obstacles. The Bible tells us, *"In all these things we are more than conquerors through him who loved us"* (Romans 8:37). What things? Life, death, angels, demons, the present, the past, the future, or anything else in the world. Those are some pretty big obstacles, but God wants to take you over them.

Overcoming Is Going Around

The movie *Soul Surfer* shows how hard it was for Bethany Hamilton to simply balance and stand up on a surfboard when she first tried it again after losing her arm. But she got past that obstacle pretty quickly. The primary challenge was with the bigger waves.

A surfer has to get behind the bigger waves in order to catch them before they break. Trying to take on a wall of moving whitewater only pushes you backward, toward the shore—or throws you into the impact zone. Surfers duck dive. That means they push their board underwater and swim *under* an incoming wave. The process of getting underwater with a

Sometimes overcoming the obstacles in our lives means asking for God's help, listening for His wisdom, and then fighting against it with all the strength He gives us.

surfboard kind of looks like ducks with their tail feathers pointing toward the sky.

Try doing *that* with one arm. It was a problem for Bethany. But her dad saw the challenge and designed a special handle that attached to her board. It gave Bethany the ability to control the board underwater. She could duck dive and get to the bigger waves she wanted to ride.

Fighting the waves didn't work against the power of the ocean. Instead, Bethany relied on others to help, got creative, and God helped her find a way around the problem. Sometimes, that's what it takes to overcome. You might have to ask God for help to adapt or change—but you can move ahead.

Overcoming Is Moving On

Genna Dodge was an athlete at heart. She loved basketball, soccer, and softball. But by the time she was twelve, Genna was faced with the reality of multiple injuries and knee surgery. She needed to overcome those injuries to get back to the things she loved. But there was no way she could play those sports while she was recovering from surgery.

That's when Genna jumped at the chance to go golfing with her grandmother. She could do that. And she discovered she loved it. Golf became her new favorite sport, and she kept playing even after her knee recovered. Genna went on to play in college at Gonzaga University. She hopes to become a pro. Watch for her on the LPGA (Ladies Professional Golf Association) tour.

Genna didn't overcome her injuries to return to things she used to love. She overcame them by refusing to let her obstacles keep her down. And she found a new love that was even better.

Sometimes, overcoming means changing routes completely. If the obstacle in your way is truly not something you can get past, you have the choice to sit there and never move forward again. Or you can ask God to show you a new road to take. It might mean discovering new passions and taking on a totally new challenge that you can succeed at. But even if you don't know what those new passions, skills, and dreams are, start taking advantage of opportunities to try new things. It's always easier for God to guide you when you are already in motion.

Overcoming Is Praying

Where do you go for the wisdom and understanding you need to overcome the obstacles in your path? By going to the One who drew up the master plan for your life and sees everything from beginning to end. The Bible says, *"Trust in the LORD with all your heart; do not depend on your own understanding. Seek his will in all you do, and he will show you which path to take"* (Proverbs 3:5–6, NLT). That's an awesome promise. God will direct your steps and show you the way to go when you seek His plan for your life.

You seek God out the same way you would seek out a friend. You talk to Him and get to know Him. What we have just described is prayer. Yeah, we get it. You've probably been hearing about prayer all your life, and you might have even thought it is some big, formal thing with lots of do's and don'ts. Actually, it's just having a conversation with God and spending time with Him. So when you come to a roadblock or detour, you can ask God about it. You can talk to Him and let Him know what you're unsure about. He has promised us that He's always listening. He's never too busy. The Bible says, *"This is the confidence we have in approaching God: that if we ask anything according to his will, he hears us"* (1 John 5:14).

And He will answer, though not always exactly like you might want or expect. But He will give you what you need. He probably won't show you the whole road ahead, but He'll give you the strength, courage, and direction to take the next step. As you do that and keep moving forward, you will be able to ride right over, through, or around your problems and challenges.

BIG-O—OVERCOMING

Ever play Rock, Paper, Scissors? It's the ultimate game for settling disagreements. It's so simple, anyone can play. Do you remember what beats what? Rock beats scissors; scissors cut paper; paper covers rock.

In life, it's the Us, Evil, Good game. And the Bible tells us what beats what. Evil tries to overcome us. But we can do good. And good overcomes evil. Romans 12:21 puts it this way, *"Do not be overcome by evil, but overcome evil with good."*

Evil was God's biggest obstacle. But He made the ultimate good-overcomes-evil move when He sent Jesus to die and rise from the dead. He conquered the power of sin and death. And He allows us to conquer it too! Riding God's wave includes joining Him in overcoming evil and enjoying the good results. We get involved in His kind of conquering, and He helps us overcome the obstacles we face in our lives.

You can overcome evil in your life everyday with simple, small choices. Some of them might look like these:

- Reach out to the lonely kid at school.
- Thank your parents for all they do for you.
- Act and talk kindly to your brothers or sisters.
- Smile more.
- Complain less.
- Take your teacher flowers.
- Shovel the snow off your neighbor's sidewalk.
- Help others, especially those who can't help themselves.

Choices like these can give you momentum on God's wave. They keep you moving forward, bringing small victories day by day. They put God's love into action and show you and others what's possible. They can keep your vision focused on Jesus. And when you're looking at Jesus, you're seeing what's much bigger and stronger than any barrier that gets in your way.

God wants to show you the way to overcome. Trust Him. Follow Him. And let Him teach you to overcome all obstacles on the way to your dream. Don't ever give up!

YOUR RIDE

Draw a picture of a mountain range. Label each peak with an obstacle you are facing in your life—something that seems like it's stopping you. Then along each of the slopes, write at least one practical step you can take to overcome it and move forward. Draw yourself on the top celebrating your conquest.

"Real difficulties can be overcome; it is only the imaginary ones that are unconquerable."

—Theodore N. Vail, US telephone industrialist

"Out of difficulties grow miracles."

—Jean de la Bruyere, French satirist

"Success is to be measured not so much by the position that one has reached in life as by the obstacles which he has overcome."

—Booker T. Washington, educator, author, and political leader

"Obstacles don't have to stop you. If you run into a wall, don't turn around and give up. Figure out how to climb it, go through it, or work around it."

—Michael Jordan, professional athlete

CHAPTER 16

DETERMINED TO SUCCEED

"I don't need easy. I just need possible."

–*Bethany Hamilton in the movie* SOUL SURFER

In the movie Soul Surfer, *there is a great scene in which Bethany learns to surf again—and not just ride the waves for fun but surf competitively! Her dad sticks a bunch of surfboards in the sand and explains that she has to go from riding the easier long board to mastering the short board surfers need to "carve" waves in a competition. As Bethany works to regain her surfing ability, she crashes over and over again, slamming into the waves and coming up with a faceful of salt water. But she doesn't give up. She just keeps getting back on the board until finally she winds up celebrating with her dad on the beach.*

Life takes determination! We've already learned that all us will experience pain, setbacks, and obstacles. To get past the tough times and succeed in life takes a strong will. Read on, and you'll meet some people who definitely have the guts and determination to keep on keeping on!

It takes determination to compete in an Ironman triathlon. You've heard of the Ironman, right? The Ford Ironman World Championship in Hawaii each year is the mother of all triathlons. Competitors swim 2.4 miles in the open ocean. Then they hop on a bike and ride 112 miles. And they top it off next by running a marathon, all 26.2 miles. That's right, 140.6 miles altogether. It's enough to make you tired just thinking about it. The Ironman takes the very best men in the world more than eight hours to finish, and the very best women more than nine hours. Some racers take the whole seventeen hours before being cut off at midnight.

It takes determination just to train, qualify, and reach the Ironman. For some even more than others. Linsey Corbin is a pro triathlete who was heading for the Ironman in Hawaii for the first time. (She had only been a pro for about a month, but she had finished seventh in a qualifying Ironman race.) However, two months before the race, Linsey encountered an obstacle. She was hit by a truck while riding her bike and ended up with her collarbone broken in four places. Completing the swimming part of the race with a broken collarbone would be a huge problem.

Determination isn't about easy. It's about possible.

With little time to recover, most racers would have given up, but Linsey did not. She was practically born with a determined streak a mile wide. When she was a baby, her first words weren't "mama" or "dada" like most babies. Hers were, "I do it." And at the Ironman in Hawaii, she did it, finishing thirtieth overall out of the seventeen hundred racers.

Want a better idea of what Linsey and other Ironman competitors go through? Here's a look at the numbers:

- **10**—The number of pounds Linsey lost during that Ironman Hawaii.
- **8**—The number of toenails Linsey lost during her first Ironman.
- **6,500**—The number of calories consumed during an Ironman (an average adult eats about 2,000 calories a day)
- **6**—The number of meals Linsey eats a day.
- **7**—The average minutes per mile she accomplished during the Ironman marathon.
- **7**—The number of days a week Linsey is happy to be a pro triathlete.

So are you ready to sign up for a triathlon? Racers like Linsey can make us think either 1) *They're crazy!* or 2) *Hey, maybe I can too!* Or maybe some of both. The greater the challenge, the more we admire the person who overcomes it. They're like the ultimate underdogs. How many times have you rooted for the underdog in a contest? They give us hope that maybe we can overcome our obstacles too. Their determination can inspire us even if we never take on the same challenges.

Maybe that's part of what makes Bethany Hamilton's story so powerful. She told her family, "I don't need easy. I just need possible" as she worked to reach her dream of becoming a professional surfer. What a great line! (That's one worth writing down and sticking on your mirror!) Determination isn't about easy. It's about possible. It drives us to imagine, fight for, and reach what can be—to go for it!

TRY

Maybe the most determined animals in the world are salmon. The fish live most of their adult lives in the ocean, but when it comes time to reproduce, the salmon follow a deep inner instinct to go back to where they were born. How do they find their way back? They somehow just know. It's like God has placed a GPS in them that drives and draws them onward. Talk about obstacles! They swim up big rivers—against the current! They have to jump up waterfalls and dodge hungry grizzly bears trying to catch and eat them. Some don't make it, but they are all driven by instinct to go for it. The salmon always keep swimming. They're determined. They never give up.

Trying makes possibility, and when you've got possibility, you've got a shot at success.

There's always a chance that we might fail when we try, but trying is what actually opens the door to success. If you want to swim across the pool, you've got to jump in the water. If you want to make the cross-country team, at some point you have to lace up your shoes and go running. If you want to be a successful musician, you have to sit down with the piano, guitar, or oboe and play. And if you want to make good grades, you have to pay attention in class and study.

You've got to keep trying. You know the old saying "If at first you don't succeed, try, try again." It has become common wisdom because it's true. And you must try with your whole heart. A half-hearted attempt will only get you halfway there, if that far. Half-hearted tries don't do much good. They're easily beaten by obstacles.

Try and keep trying. Trying makes possibility, and when you've got possibility, you've got a shot at success.

DON'T GIVE UP

Have you ever watched a dog play with a toy that has a treat inside? Talk about focus! All the dog can think of is getting at that treat. It wants it so bad. Sometimes, you wonder if it might actually die trying to reach its goal. But dogs don't die that way. They keep chewing and pawing and trying until they get what they're after. They never give up.

The Bible gives us encouragement that if we keep going the right way, we'll reach what we're aiming for too. It says, *"Be strong and do not give up, for your work will be rewarded"* (2 Chronicles 15:7). Set your mind on your dream—the thing you feel passionate about, the thing you know God has placed in your heart, the thing you can use your talents for, the thing you want more than anything else   and go for it. And keep going. Don't give up. If you feel like you can't go on, ask God to give you the grace to keep going.

Seventeen-year-old Kyle Schauvliege's dream was to go to state in cross-country. Well, back up a step, first his dream was to walk again. When Kyle was twelve, he fell off and was run over by a tractor pulling a mower on his family's Kansas farm. His leg was broken and cut up badly. Doctors told him he might spend the rest of his life in a wheelchair. Kyle had to endure surgeries and

When you're walking through your life with God, He guides and directs you, fills you with His confidence, and gives you the strength you need to keep going.

lots of physical therapy in order to get the use of his leg back. But Kyle didn't just want to walk. He wanted to run again. And he was determined.

It took a year before Kyle could walk without crutches. And he had to sit out seventh- and eighth-grade sports so that his leg could heal properly. But Kyle never gave up. Five years later, he led his team to the state championships where he finished an impressive fifth individually.

And while we're on the subject of running, you should know about Scott Jurek and the Badwater Ultramarathon. How does running from the lowest spot in the Western Hemisphere, Death Valley, to Mount Whitney—8,360 feet above sea level—sound? Oh, we should mention temperatures can hit over 120 degrees in Death Valley. And it's no short race; it's 135 miles. See, there's a reason why they call the Badwater the world's toughest footrace.

The Badwater is all about determination. You've got to really, really want it. You've got to make yourself keep going when your body is screaming at you to *stop!* But every year, one hundred runners gather at the starting line. Some don't make it. Some only compete once. Scott Jurek has won the race twice. He's a professional ultramarathoner. His passion is not only to run, but to run long, superhuman distances. The races he regularly runs and often wins are fifty miles, one hundred miles, or more. Each one is a test of Scott's determination. Every day of training reminds him to stay focused and to never give up. He doesn't, and he's living his dream.

Determination keeps us going even when we don't succeed—especially when we don't succeed.

CONFIDENCE BOOST

It's often easier to fight through the big obstacles in front of us, such as injuries, opponents, or someone saying, "You can't do it." But don't forget to watch out for the obstacles that pop up on the inside, such as self-doubt, fear, laziness, or apathy (that's not caring, or feeling unmotivated). Make no mistake, you can fight through these barriers too.

How? By reaching for confidence—not just confidence in yourself but confidence in your dream and in God, the Giver of your dream. When you're walking through your life with God, He guides and directs you, fills you with His confidence, and gives you the strength you need to keep going. The Bible says, *"I can do all things through him who strengthens me"* (Philippians 4:13 ESV).

How's that for a confidence boost, courage boost, and motivation boost? With God, you can do anything!

There was a guy in the Bible who thought he might have that kind of confidence. The man's son had been sick for years, and he had tried everything. Then he heard that a man named Jesus had touched a number of people and sent them on their way healed. He was hopeful that Jesus could do the same for his son. The man sought out Jesus and said, "Have mercy on us and help us, if you can."

Jesus took a look at him and said, "What do you mean, 'If I can'? Anything is possible if a person believes."

Mark 9:24 says *"the father instantly cried out, 'I do believe, but help me overcome my unbelief!'"* (NLT)

Do you ever feel like that? You want to believe Jesus can help you make a new friend, get on the team, or even find a dream for your life. You think He can. You've heard it's true, and you want to trust it. It's okay if your confidence is still teetering. That guy in the story shows us that we can still come to Jesus and ask for help.

Should we believe? Yes. But most important, we should ask for God's help—even help with feeling confident. Know what Jesus did for the father? He helped him. He healed his son. He made his dream come true.

REMEMBER THE JOURNEY

Determination keeps us going even when we don't succeed—especially when we don't succeed. And honestly, it usually takes lots of tries and failures and more tries to accomplish what we're dreaming of. It's in the process, though, that we learn about our dream and how to reach it and about ourselves. It's all part of the stuff He uses to make us stronger and move us forward. It's also part of how He reminds us that success isn't always what we think it will be—sometimes, it looks surprisingly different.

Don't ever forget: You can do all things through Him who gives you strength. That's a reason to never give up!

Sixteen-year-old Abby Sunderland learned some of that when she set out to become the youngest person to sail around the world alone. How's that for a big dream? Abby had been on and around boats since she was a baby, and she began sailing by herself when she was thirteen. She also got a boost of confidence when her brother Zac successfully sailed around the world. He finished when he was seventeen. Watching Zac achieve his dream made Abby think, *Hey, I can do that too!*

With her family's support and a boatload of hard work and determination, Abby set sail from California in 2010 on her boat *Wild Eyes*. She encountered some mechanical trouble early on but managed to fix it and headed south around the tip of South America and into the southern Atlantic Ocean. She cleared the bottom of Africa and was more than halfway around the world when she encountered another obstacle in the Indian Ocean—twenty-five-foot seas and seventy-mile-per-hour winds knocked her boat over and broke off its mast. Abby had no choice but to call for a rescue. She was okay, but her quest was over.

So was it a failure? It's true that Abby didn't reach her ultimate goal. But she tried. She didn't give up. She stayed determined and accomplished a lot in the process, including becoming the youngest person to ever sail successfully around Cape Horn, the most southern tip of South Africa. It's considered the Mount Everest of sailing. None of that was a failure. It was just success of a different kind. And who knows? It might be a big step for Abby on the way to reaching her big dream of making it around the world. She's obviously one determined girl. Don't be surprised if you hear about her going for an around-the-world sailing expedition again.

Determination often leads us to unexpected accomplishments that show us we can endure more and fight harder than we think. Ernest Shackleton sure learned that lesson. Shackleton was a successful sailor and explorer, but he's most famous for an expedition that didn't end up the way it was supposed to.

Shackleton set out to cross Antarctica via the South Pole in 1914. That was way before GPS satellites and airplanes and before high-tech clothes were available to keep you warm. No one had ever been to the South Pole until 1911. But Shackleton and his crew had a dream and a ship named *Endurance*. And boy, was that ever the perfect name for this expedition.

Endurance froze into the sea ice as it got close to Antarctica. The crew was trapped on their ship, but they hoped the ice might thaw enough to set them free. They lived aboard the ship for ten months, using all the supplies they had with them, only to see the ice crush the ship to pieces. The men, left floating on the ice, set sail in three lifeboats and reached Elephant Island. It was solid ground, but not a place where they could survive for long. In desperation, Shackleton took five men and set out again in one small boat. Sixteen days and eight hundred miles of open ocean later, they miraculously reached an inhabited island. Of course, the men then had to hike over some mountains to the other side of the island before they found help. But their determination paid off. A rescue party was sent back for the other crew members, who all survived. That was the most amazing success of all!

Determination means never giving up even when you feel like it. It means practicing your jump shot from the spot that you keep missing. It means playing the song over and over until you don't miss those notes. It means working that math problem until you finally get the answer.

Determination means staying focused on your goal even when obstacles pop up. It means trusting God—your ultimate source of strength—to help you keep going even when your attempts look like failures. Don't ever forget: You can do all things through Him who gives you strength. That's a reason to never give up! You don't need easy. You just need possible.

YOUR RIDE

You're good at stuff. You have gifts. And you already have many accomplishments. Sometimes, remembering what you've done before can help you feel more confident. Make a list of things you have done, awards you have won, compliments people have given you. Look it over and remind yourself, *I can do it!*

Take it a step further and memorize Philippians 4:13 and say it every morning.

"You may have to fight a battle more than once to win it."
—Margaret Thatcher, former British prime minister

"Success consists of going from failure to failure without loss of enthusiasm."
—Winston Churchill, former British prime minister

"Don't aim for success if you want it; just do what you love and believe in, and it will come naturally."
—David Frost, British journalist

"God does not give a lick of an Ice cream cone without wanting you to have the whole cone."
—Marshall Thurber, author and public speaker

PART 6

Swell on the Horizon

CATCHING GOD'S WAVE

Isaiah 55:8-9

"My thoughts are not your thoughts, neither are your ways my ways," declares the LORD. "As the heavens are higher than the earth, so are my ways higher than your ways and my thoughts than your thoughts."

1 Thessalonians 5:18

Give thanks in all circumstances, for this is God's will for you in Christ Jesus.

Luke 6:31

Do to others as you would have them do to you.

Galatians 5:14

The entire law is summed up in a single command: "Love your neighbor as yourself."

Matthew 5:16 ESV

Let your light shine before others, so that they may see your good works and give glory to your Father who is in heaven.

Philippians 2:3-4

Do nothing out of selfish ambition or vain conceit, but in humility consider others better than yourselves. Each of you should look not only to your own interests, but also to the interests of others.

CHAPTER 17
GAINING PERSPECTIVE

"So, you see how hard it can be to make sense of things when you are looking at them really close. The same thing's true in life. So, if you guys are dealing with anything that's just too hard to handle or doesn't seem to make much sense, get a new perspective."

–Sarah Hill in the movie SOUL SURFER

In the movie SOUL SURFER, there's a scene in which Bethany and her friends go to the church's RAD Night youth group meeting. Their leader, Sarah Hill, has them play a game called "Can You Tell Your Ear from Your Elbow?" The group looks at weird pictures that some of them think are a dodgeball, a blob in a lava lamp, or even a dead, rotting brain (ugh!). When Sarah zooms out on the pictures it becomes clear that the group is actually looking at a fly's eye and a walnut.

Sarah's game makes a good point, that we sometimes have to step back and get the big picture in order to make sense of life. God definitely has the big view of things, and if we try to see situations from His viewpoint, they start to make a lot more sense. In this chapter, we'll talk about how to get a whole new perspective on life.

~~~

Take a good look at the box below. What is it? Can you tell? How would you describe it to someone else?

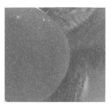

Now take a look at this box.

You might not realize this at first, but the two images are identical. The regular-size image is easy to identify. But the enlarged image is not. Our lives work a lot like this visual exercise. When some event or problem is right up in our grill, staring us in the face, it's hard to say what's up and what's down. We have to step back and look at the problem in its right perspective before we can make a good choice about what to do.

Think about being mad at a friend or a brother or sister. Maybe something they said set you off, and you're seeing red—and that's about all you're seeing. Fast forward a couple of hours, and the scene looks totally different. You're buddies again, and you can't even remember what you were so angry about. The problem that was blowing up your world is now no big deal. There's a much clearer picture when you have a different perspective.

This works in the opposite way too. When you're trying to see something far away, it can be fuzzy and unclear. Maybe you can make out a shape on the horizon. Maybe you can't see anything at all. But the closer you get, the clearer the object becomes until it's totally obvious.

You may have experienced that on a family road trip. It feels like you're driving forever and there's nothing but empty horizon ahead. Then wait— look! There's something way out there if you squint. Could it really be the mountains, the beach, or the Disneyland sign you've been watching for? You keep moving forward, and with every mile you can see it clearer and clearer until there's no mistake. Finally, you've made it.

It's all about perspective.

HERE COMES THE SWELL

Surfers make an art form out of looking for waves, and perspective makes a big difference. Look around the next time you're at the beach. You'll probably see surfers looking out to sea from the shore, a nearby cliff, or standing in the back of a pickup truck. Many will be using binoculars. The surfers want to catch the best waves possible, so they check things out from any good vantage point they can find. When they're up high and far back, they can see the big picture: what kind of waves are rolling in from far away. They need a wide-angle perspective to give them an idea of what to expect once they're in the water.

But when it comes to actually catching a wave, surfers get into the water, sit on their boards in the lineup, and look toward the horizon. If there are no waves in sight, they wait, feeling the water pushing or pulling. Their perspective is somewhat limited now because they're surrounded by water and low to the waterline, but they rely on what they saw earlier from higher ground to guide them. They draw on the information they gathered earlier: which direction the swells were coming from and where the waves were generally breaking. Now they watch and wait. When the bump of a swell appears rolling through the water toward them, they paddle. They want to be in the right place at the right time to catch the wave.

When you are listening to God, you get the benefit of His big-picture perspective.

The same is true for soul surfers. We need to get all the wisdom and advice we can gather so that we can keep a good perspective. And that's one of the biggest advantages to being in relationship with God. He sees everything. He knows everything. When you are listening to God, you get the benefit of His big-picture perspective.

Now, don't make the mistake some people make. They say they can't move toward their dream because they can't see any good waves on the horizon. They want to be a drummer, but the band at school is lame. They want to learn to ski, but they don't have money for lift tickets. They want to befriend a new student in class, but they tell themselves that person seems really cool and probably wouldn't be interested in being friends. So they do nothing, and nothing gives them no perspective at all.

Doing nothing is like sitting on the shore and waiting for that big wave. By the time you see it coming, it'll be too late to paddle out and catch it. If you want that wave, really want it, you've got to be in the water, ready and waiting.

The band may be lame, but if you get involved and learn your stuff, you'll be in a good position when a new band teacher comes to your school. If you start working at the ski shop, you'll earn some money, and you might even have the opportunity to purchase discounted lift tickets. If you try talking to that new student, you might find the best friend you've ever had, but you won't know unless you try. Taking action gives you momentum and changes your location so you're in a good position to see opportunities and seize them. Taking steps toward your dream helps the impossibilities fade and gives you new perspective on the possibilities.

CAPTURING PERSPECTIVES

Photography is all about perspective too. Pictures are frozen perspectives. If you want to have fun, get out a camera and try the exercise at the beginning of this chapter. Point the camera at a nearby object and zoom in really, really close. If you're too close, the camera image will be blurry, and you won't be able to tell what you're looking at on the display screen. Try widening the lens as far back out as you can. You'll see more objects but lose detail.

A wide-angle panoramic shot captures big stuff like majestic mountains and big crowds of people. Close-up shots focus tightly and capture details like a flower growing on a mountain or one single face in the crowd. Photos have the power to change our perspective about the world.

That's what Logan Frye hoped his pictures would do for others. Logan's perspective changed drastically when he visited New Orleans after Hurricane Katrina. The seventeen-year-old went with classmates in 2007 to help with the massive cleanup efforts after the devastating storm. Logan lived in Arizona. He hadn't thought much about hurricane victims before that trip. He was living his life, going to school, hanging out with friends.

But Logan's trip opened his eyes to a bigger world and bigger issues.

When Logan returned to Arizona, he printed and framed eighteen of his photos from New Orleans. He chose images of kitchens dripping in mold, a car buried by a house, and an Elmo puppet stuck on a fence. He titled the collection "Eyes Wide Open" and displayed it at a local coffee shop. His hope was that the images would change other people the same way his experience in New Orleans had changed him. He hoped he could help others live with their eyes wide open.

Astronomers throughout history have shared one common goal—to see more, to see farther, to see deeper into space, and to see the world from a different perspective. Recent astronomers have received a big boost from the Hubble Space Telescope. It revolutionized the kind of space images that are possible and forever changed our perspective about the universe.

The telescope has been orbiting the earth since 1990 at a speed of five miles per second. Not miles per hour—miles per *second*! That's fast enough to get across the United States in about 10 minutes! This is one impressive piece of technology. Hubble captures light from space to show scientists never-seen-before details about our universe and beyond. It has shed light on mysteries such as the collapse of stars and the birth of galaxies. This one telescope has given scientists a way of putting our planet and our universe in perspective.

Want to expand your view of God's bigness and power? Check out HubbleSite.org and look at some of Hubble's pictures from space. It might just change how you see your own life. The images are mind boggling. All this strange and incredible stuff is out there, floating and moving around—and God made it all. He wants to reach into your life, take you by the hand, and give you a bigger, clearer, much-improved perspective. *Wow* isn't nearly enough of a word to describe that!

(And if you check out the Hubble and are impressed, watch for an even more powerful infrared telescope called the James Webb Space Telescope. It's supposed to launch sometime in 2014. It should be supernova-cool.)

GIVE THANKS

Okay, let's come back to earth where you don't have the Hubble to shed light on your life. You do, however, have a powerful tool you can use every day to zoom in or out to change the angle of your life picture. It's called giving thanks. It sounds simple, but it's a powerful perspective giver.

An attitude of thankfulness forces you to focus on what you have, not on what you don't have. It's more than just saying thanks. It's a way of looking at things—a perspective—that focuses on the good in life more than the hardships.

Thankfulness is at the heart of the classic question, *Is the glass half empty or half full?* Your answer reveals your perspective. Viewing your cup of life as half-empty leads you down a path of self-pity, jealousy, and despair. But looking at the glass as half full leads you down the road of thankfulness, generosity, and hope—that's a much better road to travel.

No matter what you pick as your viewpoint, the glass in that question doesn't change. The only thing that really changes is the way you look at it. Here are a few illustrations to show you what we mean.

Your best friend gets sick and can't go to the concert. It's ruined; you can't go either (half empty). Or you're disappointed but thankful you can invite a new friend to go (half full).

Your cell phone dies when you accidentally drop it in the toilet. *Ewww.* Your connection to everyone is ruined; you can't afford a new phone right now, so your social life is doomed (half empty). Or you're bummed, but you're thankful you still have your computer to help you stay connected. And maybe you have a good allowance and a couple of regular babysitting jobs that will help you save enough money for a new phone pretty quickly (half full).

Your family is taking a trip—and it means you're going to miss the big Homecoming dance. You can't believe it! You hate it! They totally planned this to ruin your fun. It's as bad as getting sent to Siberia (half empty). Or you really are sad to miss the dance, but you're thankful you're going to get to see your cousins who live far away (half full).

Thankfulness has a way of taking your focus off yourself and your problems and putting it on God and His blessings. It's so important to be thankful that the

An attitude of thankfulness forces you to focus on what you have, not on what you don't have.

Bible says we should give thanks all the time. *"Whatever happens, keep thanking God because of Jesus Christ. This is what God wants you to do"* (1 Thessalonians 5:18 CEV).

Really? Thankful in every situation you face? Even when you're miserable? What if your heart is broken and your problems really hurt? What if you're truly being treated unfairly? What if you just don't like what's going on? How can you be thankful for those things? You don't have to be thankful *for* them, but you can be thankful *in* them. There is a difference.

Paul and Silas were two very glass-half-full kind of guys in the Bible. They knew how to be thankful no matter what. One time, they were on a mission trip when Paul commanded a spirit to come out of a demon-possessed slave girl. Her masters didn't like it because the girl earned money for them by fortune-telling. Angered by this loss of income, the men started a riot and had Paul and Silas arrested. Paul and Silas were whipped and thrown in jail.

What would you do in their shoes—besides bleed and feel pain from your wounds? Paul and Silas prayed and sang worship songs to God, loud enough for the other prisoners to hear them. They stayed thankful to God. We're sure they weren't happy about being beaten and jailed, but even in the middle of it, they kept their eyes on God instead of on their pain and suffering. (You can read the whole story in Acts 16:22–26. Their actions introduced all the prisoners to Jesus and saved the jailer's life.)

GIVE IT AWAY

Chelsea Dalton was seventeen when she said thank-you by cutting off her hair—ten inches of it! What does losing your locks have to do with being thankful? When Chelsea was only five, she was diagnosed with leukemia. She had long, beautiful blond hair at the time, but it all fell out during chemotherapy. Then someone gave her a pretty purple hat with long blond hair coming out the back. It helped Chelsea look more normal, and it meant the world to the little girl dealing with so much.

Chelsea didn't know who donated that blond hair, so she couldn't thank them personally. But as a healthy teenager, Chelsea wanted to show her thankfulness by doing the same for someone else. So she cut her hair and donated it to Locks of Love. That's an organization that makes hairpieces for cancer patients.

Sometimes, expressing thanks through our actions can actually jump-start our hearts. Doing something to show thanks to God or other people can help us see and feel a more thankful perspective.

Don't have ten inches of hair to spare? That's okay. There are tons of ways to show thankfulness. You could write a letter to deployed military troops saying thank-you for your freedom. You could give a flower to your friend to say thank-you for the listening ear when you were feeling sad. You could simply hug your mom and say thank-you for all the things she does for your family. There are a million ways to say thanks.

Write down a few ideas of your own for who and how you can show thanks.

He wants to fill your heart with joy and love that can't help but overflow with thankfulness.

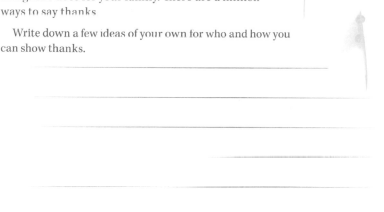

_____

_____

_____

_____

_____

However you do it, show your thankfulness and watch your perspective change as you begin to see life as full and overflowing.

FROM GOD'S PERSPECTIVE

God's glass is always full. God's eye view is always perfect. He sees differently than we do. He says, *"As the heavens are higher than the earth, so are my ways higher than your ways and my thoughts than your thoughts"* (Isaiah 55:9).

He sees the ultimate good in every situation and potential benefit in every problem. He wants to teach you how to have that perspective. He understands that your own outlook is limited. He's patient when you bumble around without grasping the big picture around you. But He doesn't want to leave you there. He wants to open your eyes so you can see your situation clearly.

One of the best parts of having a relationship with God is letting Him adjust your perspective. He wants you to see like He sees because it's the most awesome view in the universe. He wants to fill your heart with joy and love that can't help but overflow with thankfulness. And He wants to help you every step of the way—that alone is reason to give lots of thanks.

YOUR RIDE

Practice being thankful. Make a thank-you card for God or for someone who has made a difference in your life. List things you are thankful for and see how your perspective changes.

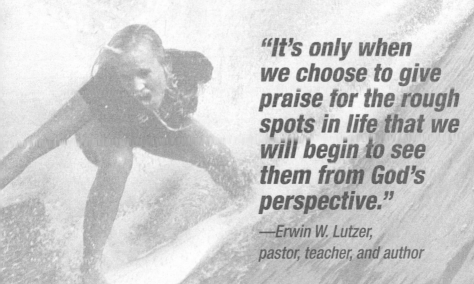

"O Lord! that lends me life,
Lend me a heart replete with thankfulness!"
—William Shakespeare, *in* King Henry VI

"In ordinary life we hardly realize that we receive a great deal more than we give, and that it is only with gratitude that life becomes rich."
—Dietrich Bonhoeffer, German theologian

"Gratitude unlocks the fullness of life. It turns what we have into enough, and more. It turns denial into acceptance, chaos to order, confusion to clarity. It can turn a meal into a feast, a house into a home, a stranger into a friend. Gratitude makes sense of our past, brings peace for today, and creates a vision for tomorrow."
—Melody Beattie, author

"It's only when we choose to give praise for the rough spots in life that we will begin to see them from God's perspective."
—Erwin W. Lutzer, pastor, teacher, and author

CHAPTER 18

PUTTING YOURSELF IN SOMEONE ELSE'S SHOES

"Don't be sorry for compassion, Bethany. It can move us to do amazing things, and it can help you get a new perspective."

–Sarah Hill to Bethany Hamilton in the movie SOUL SURFER

In the movie SOUL SURFER, Bethany decides to go on her youth group's mission trip to Thailand, which has just been badly damaged by a tsunami. There is a very touching scene in the movie in which Bethany meets a woman who tearfully says, "I lost my family. My family, they all die. I'm so sad." Bethany has been through a very painful experience, but when she meets people who have lost their homes and their families, she realizes how much she still has. As her father says, "You have a family who loves you." Stepping into the shoes of the people living in Thailand gives Bethany a whole new perspective. (You remember perspective from the last chapter, right?)

What Bethany was feeling was compassion, which means to sympathize with someone who is suffering and to want to help them. As Sarah Hill explains, compassion can lead us to action. And action can make the world a better place! Read on to meet some soul surfers who stepped into other people's shoes in a very cool way.

Mike and Sam scraped the food out of the dumpster and ate it—gladly. They were just happy for something, *anything* to eat. Food was hard to come by on the streets. Everything was hard to come by on the streets: a safe place to sleep at night, shelter during storms, money, you name it. The two young homeless men played their guitars and sang songs on the streets to scrounge up a little cash, but it wasn't much.

Would you believe this was Mike and Sam's dream? The idea had hit Mike Yankoski one Sunday: *Be the Christian you say you are.* That meant loving other people, even the lowliest of people. And it led Mike to a big and kind-of-crazy plan: become homeless, at least for a while. Why? To understand what life was like for those people and find out firsthand how the Church was meeting their needs—or not.

So Mike and his friend Sam Purvis, both college students, got advice from their parents, pastors, and leaders of homeless shelters. Then they left behind their good schools, loving families, nice cars, clean clothes, and plenty of everything and hit the streets to live for five months in six big American cities.

You've heard the expression "walk a mile in someone else's shoes"? That's what Mike and Sam did. It's just that those old, dirty, smelly shoes belonged to people who live under bridges, in tent camps, and on the streets. At the end of the five months, Mike and Sam walked off the streets and back into their comfortable lives. But the experience changed them and their faith forever. (You can read more about it in the book Mike wrote called *Under the Overpass.*)

That's the way it works with putting ourselves in someone else's shoes. It can open our eyes like never before to a whole new perspective.

WHAT IT TAKES

Don't worry. You don't have to go to the extreme like Mike and Sam did.

That's the way it works with putting ourselves in someone else's shoes. It can open our eyes like never before to a whole new perspective.

Putting yourself in someone else's shoes just means finding ways to see things from their perspective. It's trying to understand where a person is coming from or see something the way that person sees it. Here are some simple, everyday ways you can do that:

Ask questions. "What do you think?" "Why?" "You mean ...?" Those are all good ones, aimed at drawing people out and encouraging them to open up and talk about what they think and how they feel.

Listen. If you ask, then you've got to listen to the answers. It may be easier for you to talk instead of listen, but focus and think about what the other person is saying. Practice with someone from another culture or country.

Look at what the other person's life or situation is like. You might assume other people live like you do. But that's not always the case. We are all shaped differently by different surroundings. Look around at the various groups at school. Instead of judging, think about what makes them who they are.

Imagine what you would feel like in their situation. Make it a mental game. Picture yourself in their circumstance. How did you get there? What would you do? Imagine yourself in the place of the kid at school with lots of problems.

Find out what they need. Asking questions and listening will help reveal this. Sometimes, needs are obvious; sometimes, they're not. What would help a friend or a stranger?

Serve them. Give to someone else. It could be providing a drink and a snack. Or it could be going with a friend to face a situation they are dreading. It could be anything. Just give of yourself.

Seeing others' strengths, weaknesses, challenges, and struggles can help you see yourself in a new light.

Looking at life from someone else's point of view will change how you look at your own life. Listening to a friend, serving the homeless, or going to another city or country for a mission trip can help you better understand others. It can help you ride God's wave and see new ways to spread His love to the world.

REDEFINING YOUR IDENTITY

A little four-year-old girl is struggling. She can't use her arms, but she's trying to pick up a plastic ball with a scooplike tool strapped to her foot. You see her. What do you think? What do you do?

Well, in this case, nothing. Ailish Eccleston's arms are just fine. She was just testing one of the displays at an exhibit at the Please Touch Museum in Philadelphia, Pennsylvania. The accessABILITY exhibit allows people to test out and experience everyday challenges faced by the disabled. They can ride through a wheelchair obstacle course, hand-pedal a bike, learn American Sign Language phrases, type their names in Braille, and more.

But what would you have done if you had seen the little girl we just mentioned in real life? Would you try to help her? Look away? Give her some encouragement? It's hard to know how to respond when you don't understand someone's situation.

Putting yourself in someone else's shoes (or lack of them) can shape your dreams. It can help you see how to blend your passions with God's good purposes for others.

Putting yourself in another person's shoes can open your eyes to see your own identity in a new way. Seeing others' strengths, weaknesses, challenges, and struggles can help you see yourself in a new light. It can lead you to thankfulness and help you see your place in God's bigger picture.

SHAPING YOUR DREAMS

Need a new pair of shoes? What's wrong with the pair (or dozen pairs) you already own? What would it be like to go barefoot all day, every day, because you didn't own any shoes? That's why the TOMS shoe company asks people to go without wearing shoes for a whole day as part of their nationwide awareness day called One Day Without Shoes.

Does a shoe company that wants people to *not* wear shoes sound backward? Well, TOMS isn't exactly your typical shoe company. Its founder, Blake Mycoskie, was always an entrepreneur. He had started five successful companies, including a campus laundry service, and was well on his way toward fulfilling the dream of being a successful businessman. Then Blake visited Argentina and saw so many kids who had no shoes that his dream changed. It shifted with his perspective. Blake could see that running around with no shoes increased the kids' risk for injury and disease, and he wanted to help.

But instead of starting a charity, Blake did what he does best—he started a business. And he built it on a one-for-one principle. For every pair of shoes TOMS sells, one pair would be donated to a child in need. TOMS has donated more than six hundred thousand pairs of shoes.

Putting yourself in someone else's shoes (or lack of them) can shape your dreams. It can help you see how to blend your passions with God's good purposes for others. It can change the rest of your life and the lives of others.

The movie *Soul Surfer* depicts the real frustration and discouragement that Bethany Hamilton suffered while trying to come back after her shark attack. It was hard to surf with one arm. She couldn't compete as well as she could before the attack. Everything was different, and her dream of becoming a professional surfer felt out of reach. She was ready to quit. Bethany's problems were way close up and hard to see through.

She had all but given up on surfing when she decided to go on a mission trip to Thailand. That Asian country had been blasted by a tsunami that killed almost a quarter of a million people. Bethany saw the devastation firsthand and met people whose whole families had died in the disaster, their homes and lives swept away by the raging water.

Bethany reached out to the Thai people and served them. She realized that the kids hadn't gone into the ocean since the tsunami because they were afraid. So she drew them out into the water and even taught some of them to surf. Her efforts helped them rediscover a once-familiar source of joy.

And while she was helping others, Bethany's perspective began to change. She saw all that others had lost and recognized all she still had. She put herself in other people's shoes, and a new view of her own life and her own dream emerged.

IGNITING YOUR COMPASSION

Shifra Mincer grew up in New York City. It's a huge city, and Shifra was used to seeing the realities of homelessness around her every day. But could she do anything to help?

A teacher offered to take students to help out at a homeless shelter for several weeks after school, so Shifra went. Maybe she could help after all. Because she knew how to sew, Shifra was asked to help repair clothes for the homeless people. Even when the school group stopped going, Shifra kept going and she kept sewing. She got to know the regulars at the shelter by mending their tattered clothing. She listened to their stories as she fixed holes in their jackets or shirts. It helped her put herself in their shoes, and she found out they were just regular people who had fallen on hard times. She also learned that they had holes not only in their clothes, but also in their hearts. They were longing for love and hope.

Helping homeless people lit a passion in Shifra that went beyond that one homeless shelter. She started a sewing club in high school to teach other people how to serve the homeless with needles and thread. Later, she volunteered with the student-run homeless shelter at her college.

Putting yourself in someone else's shoes helps you to see their humanity. And coming face-to-face with their tears, problems, hard work, pain, and joy, like Bethany and Shifra did, stirs up compassion inside you. Compassion makes you want to help. The whole process shifts your perspective, as if you were zooming in or out with the camera lens.

We all can love other people better when we identify with them and try to understand what their lives are like. God wants His soul surfers to love other people. It's really, really important to Him. In fact, it's the second-most-important priority He wants us to have. Jesus said, *"'You must love the LORD your God with all your heart, all your soul, all your strengthm and all your mind.' And, 'Love your neighbor as yourself'"* (Luke 10:26-28 NLT). Love fuels God's wave.

You don't have to go across the ocean or across town to love other people, you can start by walking across the hall. Sometimes, the people you're closest to can be the hardest to love. You might not feel like putting yourself in your brother's or sister's shoes. You might be frustrated with your parents because it feels like they always say no and they seem to be overly concerned with

> **You don't have to go across the ocean or across town to love other people, you can start by walking across the hall.**

things like chores and keeping your room clean. That leaves you not wanting to understand their point of view. But if you're willing to love them and try to understand, your family can give you a whole new perspective, showing you how God can use them to inspire and shape your dreams.

Try it with friends and classmates too. Find ways to serve them and serve *with* them. They can help you stay on track as you move forward on God's wave.

YOUR RIDE

Take a walk in someone else's shoes. Write down a few names, and answer these questions about them:

I just don't get _____

What's that person's problem? Really, think about it.

_____

_____

What would it be like to live that person's life?

_____

_____

What's one way you can reach out in love to that person?

_____

_____

How do you think it could expand your perspective?

_____

_____

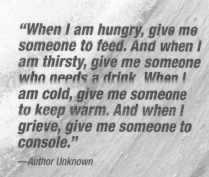

"Kindness is a language which the deaf can hear and the blind can see.
—Mark Twain, author

I shall not pass this way again: Then let me now relieve some pain, Remove some barrier from the road, Or brighten some one's heavy load.
– Eva Rose York, composer

"When I am hungry, give me someone to feed. And when I am thirsty, give me someone who needs a drink. When I am cold, give me someone to keep warm. And when I grieve, give me someone to console."
—Author Unknown

CHAPTER 19

INSPIRING OTHERS

"There's an eighth grader from North Carolina who lost his arm. Logan. And he says he's trying out for his soccer team because of me."

–Bethany Hamilton in the movie SOUL SURFER

In the movie SOUL SURFER, when Bethany returns from her mission trip to Thailand, she finds a surprise waiting for her at home. Her brothers are sorting through piles and piles of letters from people who have been inspired by Bethany's story. At first, she can't understand why they would write when she blew it at her last competition. Then her mom explains something very important: "You tried." Because Bethany was willing to keep going, and because she had the determination to get back on her board and go back in the water and even to try to compete, her unwavering faith and courage inspired others.

You might not realize it, but what you do matters—and matters very much— to other people. Each one of us can be an example to those around us. By caring. By reaching out. By trying. In this chapter, you'll meet some people who inspire others through the way they live their lives. Maybe you could be one of them!

~~~

Matt Moniz could write one heck of a "What I Did on My Summer Vacation" essay. In 2010, the rising sixth-grader and his dad visited all fifty states and climbed to the highest point in each. And they set a record by doing it in forty-three days, two hours, and nine minutes—faster than anyone ever had.

The journey began with the hardest peak, Alaska's Mount McKinley, or Denali as it's called in the native Alaskan language. That mountain is 20,320 feet tall, the highest in North America. But that didn't mean everything else was all downhill. Other high points, as they're officially called, meant Matt had to hike many miles into wilderness just to reach them. And his favorite, Gannett Peak in Wyoming, was almost a full rock climb. But others, such as Florida's 345-foot Britton Hill, just took a short run from the road up a hill.

Matt's accomplishment made the news, and he was even nominated as one of *National Geographic's* 2010 Adventurers of the Year. Lots of people asked Matt why he did it. His main reason was to raise money and awareness for his best friend, Ian Hess. Ian has a rare heart and lung disease called pulmonary arterial hypertension. Matt's adventure raised twenty-five thousand dollars for Ian and awareness to help find a cure for the disease.

Another goal Matt had was to inspire other kids to get outside, explore, and help protect American's public lands—you know, national parks and forests and wilderness areas. The young adventurer is an ambassador for Outdoor Nation. He took a day in the middle of his high-point quest to share his inspirational message with teens and kids in New York City's Central Park about the importance of getting outside and living a healthy life.

Matt really is an inspiration. He's willing to put down the game controller and head outside. It's definitely fun for him, but he doesn't do it just for himself. He's willing to share his journey to encourage other people.

Who inspires you? What is it about someone's story that stirs your heart and gets you fired up? Maybe that person has done something you would like to do. Maybe their accomplishment sounds cool or interesting. Maybe it's someone you know well, or it could be someone you've never met.

Maybe you are one of the many who were inspired by Bethany Hamilton's story. If so, you aren't alone. Her tragedy and brave fight to recapture her dream touched millions of people she

And in a world filled with people who often choose giving up over trying, Bethany stood out.

It can be one individual doing or being something good, healthy, and a little bit different— somebody willing to go past "I can't" to imagine "I can."

didn't even know. It didn't take long before piles of mail were arriving for her, including get-well wishes and thank-yous from others who had been inspired by her courage.

Bethany was surprised at first by that kind of outpouring. She hadn't achieved her dream yet. She hadn't won her contests yet. She was still just trying to get back to her dream of surfing, becoming a pro, and getting her life back on track. But Bethany inspired people because she tried. She never quit. And in a world filled with people who often choose giving up over trying, Bethany stood out. She reminded people that they could go for their dreams. She showed others that the hard times and tragedies don't have to make us give up. She made people realize that if she could try to surf again while the whole world paid attention, maybe, just maybe, others could begin to try to reach for their own dreams one more time.

INSPIRING IN LITTLE WAYS

A story—any story, *your* story—doesn't have to be huge or dramatic to be inspiring. Big stories often attract the attention of the media, but an inspiring story doesn't have to involve a world record or a trauma. We're inspired every day by people who faithfully make good choices and keep trying. We're inspired by a kind word, an honest answer, a listening ear, an encouraging hug, and a choice to look out and include others.

You've heard of peer pressure, right? It usually gets talked about as a bad thing. It's usually about a big group of people encouraging an individual to join into an action or attitude that's negative or unhealthy. You know how it works. It's the "Come on, everybody's doing it" mentality that you might get about cheating, lying, putting a person down, or even drinking, drugs, or sex.

But inspiration is like a positive peer pressure. Or think of it as peer pressure in reverse. It can be one individual doing or being something good, healthy, and a little bit different—somebody willing to go past "I can't" to imagine "I can."

Cheyenne Little is a teenage soul surfer who inspires people every day as a volunteer at the YMCA near her home in Ohio. She works at the front desk and checks people in. Pretty basic job, right? But she always does it with a big smile and a positive attitude that's contagious. Cheyenne was born with spina bifida, a condition that causes her to use a wheelchair. But she appreciates what she has instead of dwelling on what she doesn't. She says her faith in God gives her the strength to do it.

Cheyenne actually applied for the job because she was feeling so bad about herself. But when she found out she got it, she found new confidence. Cheyenne won't win any national championships of any sort, but her attitude inspires other people to appreciate all they have in life too.

Did you ever have a lemonade stand when you were a kid? Frannie Monahan had her first one in the front yard when she was five. But since then, she's taken it to a new level. With the help of her family and friends, Frannie started doing Lemon-Aid stands, which raise money for charities. When she was fifteen, she set one up at an art festival to benefit Doctors Without Borders, an organization that brings medical care to areas of the world that don't have any.

Frannie and her family squeezed fifty pounds of fresh lemons for that one. They knew they weren't going to solve world poverty by themselves, but the simple math is inspiring: one single lemon gives you six cups of lemonade, and selling each cup for one dollar is enough money to feed six kids for a day. The way Frannie sees it, a little lemon, sugar, and water can help change the world a little bit at a time.

Do you ever feel like your problems and the problems in the world around you are too big for you? That's a good time to take a look at what some other kids have done. They're inspiring because they don't see all they *can't* do. Sometimes, they just see what could be done and do it. They live a little bit like Frodo Baggins in the *Lord of the Rings* trilogy. Remember this line from that movie and book: "Even the smallest person can change the course of the world." What? You don't believe it?

Meet Vita Castria. She was six years old when she saw a Heifer International catalog at her grandmother's house. When

You can and should be inspired by them, but God made them to be who they are and you to be who you are.

she discovered that people could give money to buy food and supplies for poor people around the world, she had an inspired idea. Instead of asking for birthday gifts, she chose to ask for money—not money she could spend, but money she could give to help people. Vita raised $180, enough to buy a goat, a flock of geese, a flock of ducks, and a flock of chickens that would give people desperately needed milk, eggs, meat, and nutrition.

FINDING INSPIRATION

Those are inspiring stories. Those are real people, teens, and kids who are inspiring just because they've chosen to go after big dreams in little ways. But you don't have to do what they're doing. In fact, you shouldn't do what they're doing. You can and should be inspired by them, but God made them to be who they are and you to be who you are.

Remember from early in this book when we talked about you being God's masterpiece? He gave you unique gifts, talents, and personality; He uses those to fuel your dreams. You don't have to give away your birthday presents or work at the YMCA or hike to the high points of all fifty states. That's not the point. The point is that you can be inspired by others to be the person God created you to be. What do all those stories inspire you to do or be? Not all the people who wrote to Bethany Hamilton wanted to go surfing, but they were inspired by her story to grab hope for their own lives and to stay determined to overcome their own struggles.

So what's your thing? What do you love to do? What gifts do you have? Look for people around you who share your passion. Find out who else is doing something in that area. Look for inspiration in their stories and experiences. You can learn a lot and find great inspiration.

Jedidiah is a clothing company in California, but its

Inspiration works like a light. Turn it on, and it shines on everything around it. It brightens things up and inspires people to do more and be more.

owners and workers don't just want to make lots of money and get everyone to wear their T-shirts and hoodies. They wouldn't mind that, of course, but they're hoping for something even more. They want to inspire people.

See, the people at Jedidiah love art and fashion. Those are their passions, but their dream is to use art and fashion to help others. They have one series of T-shirts called the Hope Collection that partners with different aid organizations and ministries, such as Invisible Children and World Vision. So the Jedidiah artists create cool designs, and every time someone buys one of those shirts, Jedidiah donates ten dollars. Since 2004, they've given almost four hundred thousand dollars. It's inspiring that a clothing company can be a creative example of helping others.

Music is inspiring. It can pump you up and change your mood. Creating something with that kind of power is a gift musicians have; and it makes lots of musicians famous. Some artists only care about their fame and fortune. But other artists hope they can use the attention they get to inspire people to do more than download their songs. You can probably think of many. Bono of U2 has started several big campaigns and organizations, including One, Data, and Red, to tackle major problems in the world like hunger, poverty, HIV/AIDS, and international debt. Those are all big topics, but Bono hopes his fame and music will inspire people to get connected and help.

Every year, the band Switchfoot hosts a music and surfing festival in San Diego to raise money for Standup for Kids, a group helping kids living on the streets. Natalie Grant, Jeremy Camp, Hawk Nelson, Superchick, Hillsong United, Third Day, Tobymac, MercyMe, and many, many others point their fans to Compassion International or World Vision, two groups providing education, nutrition, and spiritual hope to poor kids around the world.

YOUR STORY, WHOSE GLORY?

What's your story? It may never be featured in a magazine, on the news, or in a feature-length film. But there's a good chance you have a Facebook page or some other social-network page, and you can use it to blog, tweet ,or post pictures or videos of what you're doing. You can touch lives right where you are by inspiring them with your story. And all media aside, you can inspire other people and make a difference in their lives—just by being you and connecting with others.

Inspiration works like a light. Turn it on, and it shines on everything around it. It brightens things up and inspires people to do more and be more. Jesus said, *"Let your light shine before men, that they may see your good deeds and praise your Father in heaven"* (Matthew 5:16). He wants to help you become an inspiration to others. Whether you ever become famous or not, He wants your life to point others to Him.

Following God's purpose for your life is inspiring because it encourages others to reach for their own potential. It dares them to imagine what soul surfing with the God who made and gifted them can be like. It reminds them to dream and pursue their dreams. And it points them back to the God who is the source of all inspiration.

Are you inspired? Let others know and inspire them too!

YOUR RIDE

What or who has been inspiring you lately? What does it make you want to do? What does it show you? What does it make you dream of? Write down your answers and then share your inspiration with someone else. Tell them in person or use your social network. Pass on the inspiration.

"When you do the common things in life in an uncommon way, you will command the attention of the world."

—George Washington Carver, scientist and inventor

"Sometimes our light goes out but is blown into flame by another human being. Each of us owes deepest thanks to those who have rekindled this light."

—Albert Schweitzer, theologian, philosopher, and physician

"Learn and grow all you can; serve and befriend all you can; enrich and inspire all you can."

—William Arthur Ward, author and pastor

"I am only one, but I am one. I cannot do everything, but I can do something. And I will not let what I cannot do interfere with what I can do."

—Edward Everett Hale, author and historian

CHAPTER 20

HELPING OTHERS MAKE THEIR COMEBACK

"Who would've thought that teaching a kid to surf would teach me that surfing isn't the most important thing in the world and that something else is. Love."

–Bethany Hamilton in the movie SOUL SURFER

There's an amazing scene in the movie SOUL SURFER *when Bethany meets a little boy who has been badly affected by the tsunami. He shows up at the relief village a few days after the tsunami, and he won't talk or even smile. When Bethany realizes that he and the other villagers won't go back in the water, she wants to help them overcome their fear. With persistence, an outstretched hand, and a friendly smile, Bethany is finally able to coax the little boy into the water, onto the board, and on his way toward a comeback.*

Comebacks are not so easy. What helps is to see that someone else has gone before you, and that they have been able to overcome their pain and fear and keep going. Maybe you could be part of the solution and help other people get past a painful experience. Read on to learn about some soul surfers who did exactly that.

Greg Mortenson was climbing a mountain to honor his beloved sister who had died, and he had chosen the world's hardest mountain, K2. Also called the savage peak, K2 is the world's second highest mountain (28,251 feet) and often considered the deadliest. It almost took the life of one of the climbers in Greg's group. A heroic rescue by the team saved him, but it left Greg completely exhausted. And they still had to hike fifty miles back to the closest town.

Somewhere along the way, Greg was separated from the others, and he got lost. Disoriented and desperate, he eventually wandered into a tiny high-altitude village in Pakistan. The people there showed him great kindness and helped him regain his strength. During his stay, Greg noticed how little the villagers had. They had no medical care, and the children were malnourished. They also had no school building. Sometimes, a teacher came to the village and the children practiced math and spelling by writing in the dirt. Greg promised the village leader that he would build them a school. He didn't know how, but he knew he had to do it.

Back home in California, Greg worked on and off as a nurse to get money to climb. So getting enough funding and donations to build a school in the middle of nowhere in Pakistan was a huge undertaking. Then getting the building supplies to the small mountain village meant that lumber, tools, and everything else needed to build a school had to be carried for miles up a steep mountain on men's heads and backs. Add to that the political climate of the country at the time, and Greg had a huge challenge. But then, almost miraculously, the school took shape. The tiny village of Korphe had helped Greg make his comeback in life. He tried to do the same for them.

That one school was only the beginning of Greg's work. Other villages wanted schools, and Greg kept working to find resources to get them built. By early 2011, his Central Asia Institute had built 171 schools in Pakistan and Afghanistan. That means more than

It's like you get to stand in the water and give someone a push on their soul-surfing board that launches them into a wave they thought they'd never catch again.

CATCHING GOD'S WAVE FOR YOUR LIFE

68,000 kids, mostly girls, were given a chance for an education. And that meant they had a chance to beat poverty and oppression.

Greg's passion for rock and mountain climbing helped him pursue his dream of education and peace for a region of the world that doesn't offer much of either.

YOUR TURN

This chapter is about the fun part. It's about getting to be part of a solution, part of making the world a better place. You get to help others make their comeback, overcome their obstacles, and reach for their dreams. It's like you get to stand in the water and give someone a push on their soul-surfing board that launches them into a wave they thought they'd never catch again. You get to hoot and holler and cheer as they make their comeback.

Helping others overcome their biggest challenges is not the same as inspiration. Inspiring others happens simply when people hear or see what you're doing and think, *That's cool. I want to be like that. Maybe I could ...* But actually helping others make their comeback means being in relationship with people—challenging, encouraging, and helping them. It means making the choice to take action and follow God every day to make the world a better place and someone else's life a better story.

Your community can give you strength and help as you help others.

Sometimes, people get excited about helping other people make a comeback that's similar to one they've made themselves. That can be a good place to start, but it's not a requirement. No matter who you are, how old you are, where you are in life, or what you have or haven't experienced, you can look around at your family and friends, your school, your neighborhood, your community, and even your world and see someone with a need. And you can take action to help others get back in the water and start catching waves as a soul surfer. Start with your friends.

BACK ON THE BOARD

Jesse Billauer could never have made his comeback without his friends. Jesse was a seventeen-year-old with a promising pro surfing career ahead of him when his head slammed into the ocean floor during a wipeout. His spinal cord snapped, and he became a quadriplegic. But it didn't take long for Jesse to focus on a double dream: surf again and help other people achieve their passions.

Even your small actions can help launch others toward their dreams and possibilities.

So Jesse reached out to some friends who were pro surfers. They literally helped him get back in the water. They took him surfing, pulling him on his board out into the water and then pushing him into the waves. Jesse relearned to surf by shifting his weight while lying down on a board with special handles. He was back! But there was more.

Jesse started the Life Rolls On Foundation. He and other paralyzed ambassadors visit accident victims to encourage and inspire them. He reminds others of the joy of simply being alive. And he still partners with his friends in pro surfing. At some pro contests, they take many paralyzed people surfing for the first time, providing them with some fun and a step on their way back into life.

Reach out to the people around you. We all get strength from a community of others around us giving support and help. Your community can give you strength and help as you help others.

COMMITTED TO COMMUNITY

Shin Fujiyama couldn't do what he does without help. Shin is committed to giving people in Honduras a second chance. Much of his motivation comes from the second chance he was given as a child. When Fujiyama was young, doctors in Japan discovered a hole in his heart and didn't think he would live long. But the hole somehow closed and healed. He grew up healthy and went on to college in the United States. During his sophomore year, he traveled to Honduras and discovered his dream: to help the people there make a comeback from poverty and the destruction left over from Hurricane Mitch, which had struck the country almost ten years earlier. Together with his younger sister, Cosmo, Shin started a grassroots campaign to help build schools, houses, provide water and sanitation, and send girls to college in Honduras.

Fujiyama has come a long way from the first meeting at his college to tell other students about his campaign—only two people came. But Fujiyama kept fighting for the cause he believed in. By 2011 his organization, Students Helping Honduras, has spread to one hundred universities and high schools and raised more than one million dollars through bake sales, car washes, and small donations. They also organize service trips for students to go to Honduras and be part of the hands-on work of rebuilding a community.

CREATING OPPORTUNITY

Oral Lee Brown's life, and the lives of twenty-three children, were changed by a simple trip to the grocery store—the grocery store where a little girl asked her for a quarter. Oral Lee didn't have change, so she invited the girl to come inside to pick out any one thing she wanted. She thought the girl would pick some candy—instead, she chose a loaf of bread. Oral Lee couldn't forget the little girl and tried to find her the next day at the local elementary school. She never found the girl, but Oral Lee found a whole first-grade class full of kids like her—full of potential, but lacking opportunity.

Instead of looking at what couldn't be done, Oral Lee jumped in and never looked back. She adopted the class of twenty-three students and promised that if they stayed in school, she would pay for their college. This was a big promise! Oral Lee wasn't a millionaire looking for a way to get rid of money. She was a real estate agent who earned an average salary. She started saving right away to fulfill her promise. Not only that, she took action—she became a tutor and mentor, met with parents, and tracked each child's attendance and grades. She not only inspired them but regularly encouraged and challenged them. In 2003 and 2004, Oral Lee attended graduations at nine different colleges. Nineteen of those original first-graders went to college and three to trade schools. Many of these students say it never would have happened without Oral Lee's generosity and commitment.

What do you see when you look around you? Do you see people with problems they need help overcoming? You don't have to pay for college, but you could pay for someone's lunch and be there to listen. You could become a tutor for someone in your class or volunteer as a mentor to younger kids. Even your small actions can help launch others toward their dreams and possibilities.

EXTRAORDINARILY ORDINARY

When Joshua Guthrie looked around, he was disturbed by the fact that 3.3 million people—many of them children—die each year from diseases transmitted through unclean drinking water. Even more disturbing was the fact that almost half those kids die from what we consider an annoying illness: simple diarrhea. But what could a sixteen-year-old in Tennessee do about it? Joshua had heard of organizations that dig wells for communities around the world, but there was no way he could pay the ten thousand dollars it cost. Still, he couldn't shake the feeling that he needed to do something about it.

Joshua decided he could get other teens to help. He started a Web site, DollarForADrink.org. The idea was simple: Challenge other teens to give up one drink and give the dollar they would have spent to help build one well in Sudan. Did it work? By the time he got ready to write a check, Joshua had raised more than $5,500. The project was a success because so many people gave small amounts. Joshua took a step in the right direction, and God did the rest as other people responded. "I'm just a completely ordinary guy," Joshua says, "but I serve an extraordinary God." Joshua didn't stand back and watch; he got involved. And the people of a community in Sudan got a desperately needed well that transformed their lives and helped them make a comeback from water-related diseases.

HOW CAN I HELP?

Soul surfers see a need and do what they can to help. The

Giving and helping others keeps getting passed on— sometimes back to us, sometimes on to others, and sometimes both.

Bible tells us, *"Those of us who are strong and able in the faith need to step in and lend a hand to those who falter, and not just do what is most convenient for us. Strength is for service, not status. Each one of us needs to look after the good of the people around us, asking ourselves, 'How can I help?'"* (Romans 15:1–2 MSG). When we're strong, we can help those who are weaker. That doesn't mean we have to have it all together or have no problems of our own. It just means we should be willing to be there for someone else.

What's your step? What need do you see? Start with something you know you can handle. You don't even have to start a campaign like Joshua did— you could begin with giving up a drink and sending a dollar.

Why should we bother helping others? Sure, it might make their lives better, but it often takes our time and energy. What's in it for us? Actually, it depends on what we give. Jesus said, *"Give, and you will receive. Your gift will return to you in full—pressed down, shaken together to make room for more, running over, and poured into your lap. The amount you give will determine the amount you get back"* (Luke 6:38 NLT). Like some of the stories in this chapter, giving and helping others keeps getting passed on—sometimes back to us, sometimes on to others, and sometimes both. The soul-surfing way of life is a giving way of life, and part of that is being connected to other people, sharing support, and building greater strength together.

If you've given your heart to Jesus and are trusting God with your life, reaching out to help others make their comeback can also help you grow closer to Him. Looking into the faces of friends or strangers as you serve can help you experience God and His love in action.

RESOURCES AND PARTNERS

Need someone to partner with? There are many solid and reputable organizations doing great work. Check these out for starters:

- World Vision—WorldVision.org
- Compassion International—compassion.com
- Samaritan's Purse—SamaritansPurse.org
- Living Water International—water.cc
- Blood:Water Mission—BloodWaterMission.com

START TODAY

Need a place to start? These ideas just scratch the surface, but try them and come up with some of your own.

- Call or hang out with a friend you know has been struggling.
- Start a text-a-day with short encouragement for someone trying to come back.
- Smile at the new kid at school and say hi.
- Make and sell jewelry, lemonade, art, or whatever you're good at. Donate the funds to a favorite charity.
- Collect art supplies, sports gear, or books to donate to an orphanage or homeless shelter.
- Sponsor a child. Write to your sponsored child.
- Offer to babysit for a single mom.
- Tutor classmates or younger kids.
- Make snack bags to give to homeless people.
- Collect coats to give to low-income families.
- Organize a charity concert with a favorite local band.
- Go cheer on a friend at her game or recital.

YOUR RIDE

Who do you know who needs a comeback? Look around at your friends and your school. Who needs a hug and some encouraging words? Write down some names and simple actions you can take to help.

Now go a little bigger. Is there an organization in your neighborhood or city that is fighting an uphill battle? Do you know of a need in some other country? Add those to your list, along with an action step you can take to help. If you think helping might include a mission trip, check out Youth With a Mission—ywam.org.

"How wonderful it is that nobody need wait a single moment before starting to improve the world."

—Anne Frank

"An effort made for the happiness of others lifts above ourselves."

—Lydia M. Child, abolitionist and women's rights activist

"There is a loftier ambition than merely to stand high in the world. It is to stoop down and lift mankind a little higher."

—Henry Van Dyke, author

PART 7

Catching God's Wave for Your Life

CATCHING GOD'S WAVE

Proverbs 3:5–6

Trust in the LORD with all your heart and lean not on your own understanding; in all your ways acknowledge him, and he will make your paths straight.

1 Timothy 4:12

Don't let anyone look down on you because you are young, but set an example for the believers in speech, in life, in love, in faith and in purity.

Psalm 93:4

Mightier than the thunder of the great waters, mightier than the breakers of the sea—the LORD on high is mighty.

Romans 15:13

May the God of hope fill you with all joy and peace as you trust in him, so that you may overflow with hope by the power of the Holy Spirit.

Ephesians 3:17–19

I pray that you, being rooted and established in love, may have power... to grasp how wide and long and high and deep is the love of Christ, and to know this love that surpasses knowledge—that you may be filled to the measure of all the fullness of God.

Luke 18:27 NLT

He replied, "What is impossible for people is possible with God."

CHAPTER 21

GOING WITH THE FLOW

*"When the time is right, you'll know. Till then, you pray.
You listen. ... For what comes next."*

—Tom Hamilton to Bethany Hamilton in the movie SOUL SURFER

In the movie SOUL SURFER, *when Bethany is feeling discouraged and ready
to give up, her father comes and sits beside her on the beach. We know dads
should be totally wise and experienced, but not even Tom Hamilton knows
what's next for Bethany. What he does know is that God can lead her in
exactly the right direction. In that scene Bethany's dad encourages her to
reach out to God and to listen for His directions.*

*We know that it sometimes feels better to be in control, to think we know
exactly what we're doing and where we're going. The bad news is that feeling
isn't real, because as humans we can't know or control everything in our lives.
The good news is that God can, and if you choose to follow Him, amazing
things will happen. Read on to check out some inspiring stories of people who
went soul surfing on God's wave.*

Megan Dean was only ten when she found out she was losing her eyesight.
It was scary, understandably, but she immediately started making plans
to qualify for a guide dog. Eight years later, she finally got the dog she'd
dreamed of from Guide Dogs for the Blind: a yellow lab–golden retriever
mix named Tatiana.

Megan and Tatiana had to get to know each other like any friends do. Even more, they had to adjust to working and living together. That took developing trust. Megan says the hardest part was giving up control and letting Tatiana guide her. But when she learned to do that, she gained freedom, independence, confidence, and safety. Oh, and a new best friend.

Following God can be a little bit like having a guide dog. When Jesus left the earth, He sent the Holy Spirit to be our helper and guide. It might sound a little weird to compare the Holy Spirit to a guide dog, but there are many similarities in the way we have to learn to trust someone to see the path ahead when we cannot. People with a guide dog still have to walk and make choices. They know they have help from their canine companions, but they have to pay close attention to them. Their dogs don't speak to them out loud, but they do gently nudge, direct, and protect them. And blind people have to absolutely trust what their dogs communicate.

When you follow God's leading, you also have to make choices and put one foot in front of the other even when you can't see what's going on around you. The awesome thing you can rely on is that God *can* see what you can't, and His Spirit will gently nudge, guide, direct, and protect you. He knows how to get you safely to your dreams. You just have to learn to let go of your doubts and fears and pay attention to His cues.

And don't forget the most amazing part: He also wants to be your best friend!

GO WITH IT

Now that we've talked about trusting God's guidance, let's talk about how we should go about doing what He tells us.

When a surfer takes off on a wave, he's committed, and he's flowing with the force and energy of the water. He's not sure exactly where it will take him or what possibilities it holds, but he adjusts as he goes. It's no good to try to fight the ocean's power, but letting it carry him along can be the ride of his life.

The awesome thing you can rely on is that God can see what you can't, and His Spirit will gently nudge, guide, direct, and protect you.

Going with the flow of God's leading is life's greatest adventure, but it takes time and patience.

Riding God's wave works the same way. When you receive His guidance, you have to actively begin to move forward in the direction He has indicated and let Him carry you along. You listen carefully, paying attention to His cues. You won't know exactly where He's leading you, but you will get there. And what an adventure you'll have along the way.

Another important thing to remember when you are committed to riding God's wave to your dream is to choose the waterway carefully. The wrong waves or currents can carry you farther from God's destinations, but when you listen, He'll help you navigate the way.

Brother and sister Jay and Shannon Rau found out a lot about going with the flow and choosing their waterway wisely when they went kayaking. This was no ordinary hour-long paddle around the lake. Jay and Shannon paddled for five weeks, from Hamburg, Michigan, to Avon by the Sea, New Jersey—900 miles! The journey took them across Lake Erie, down the Erie Canal and the Hudson River, and through New York City to New Jersey.

So was it a simple float downstream? Nope. Shannon and Jay had a lot of water to cover, a lot of *moving* water. They made their plans based on following the currents, tides, and flows of the different waterways. Sometimes, they paddled. Sometimes, they used a sail connected to both boats to catch the wind and carry them more smoothly. Sometimes, they had to stop and wait; otherwise they would be wasting time and energy fighting tides and upstream currents that were much stronger than they were. Shannon and Jay basically had to follow the lead of the water and let it carry them along. By going with its flow, they made it all the way to fulfilling their kayaking dream.

PRAYING PUSHES US FORWARD

Going with the flow of God's leading is life's greatest adventure, but it takes time and patience. It often seems to us like it would be much easier to blast ahead with a supersized motor boat. We can feel frustrated sometimes when we're waiting on God to show us the way, to give us a dream, or to lift us up onto His wave for our lives. Stay patient. And don't forget that there's always one action you can take: pray.

Pray? Action? Exactly. You may have the wrong idea about prayer. You may think it's boring. You may think of it as a last resort—like you've got to do something to fix your problems or make your dreams happen right now. But that's really a backward way to think about it.

Prayer is the most powerful action we can take. *Huh?* Yeah, because it's talking directly to God, the most powerful, perfect One in the universe—the only One who can truly change or make things happen for you. He will fill you with His strength, hope, comfort, and even patience and give you what you need. And as you listen to Him in prayer, He'll guide you.

The Bible tells us to pray all the time (1 Thessalonians 5:17). That's right—never stop praying. How do you even do that? Seems like you'd need to talk to someone else some time. But this isn't about being on your knees 24-7. It's more about making a habit of talking to God about what's going on in your life. It's about checking in with God throughout your day and paying attention when He says something to your heart. How often do you check your Facebook page or get texts from friends just to keep in touch? It's kind of like that.

One of the best ways to build a habit of constant communication with God is to pray while you're doing something active. It can make prayer seem a lot less boring or sleepy too. Try it. Talk to God while you walk or run. If you love music, sing your prayers to God. If you love to write, write them out. If you love art, pray while you're covering a canvas in color. TRIBE is a group of drummers in Oklahoma who get together to pray and focus on God while they pound their drums

In the same way that you can text a friend all day throughout the day, you can carry on a conversation with God that doesn't end.

together in an empty warehouse. They say rhythm is the best language they know to use to connect their hearts with God's.

You can pray while you're riding the bus, riding your bike, driving a car, waiting for class to start, or lying in bed. Post some reminders in your locker or on your mirror that remind you to say hello to and thank God. In the same way that you can text a friend all day throughout the day, you can carry on a conversation with God that doesn't end.

But don't just talk, listen. Nobody wants a monologue from a friend. We want dialogue—a conversation that goes both ways. God speaks to us through His Word, other people, our experiences, books (like this one— hey, imagine that!), silence, and that still small voice. *That what?* You know, it's that tugging at your heart that you can't ignore that points you in the direction you should go. It's an inner voice saying, "Hey, it's this path over here. The one your friend is tempting you toward is going the wrong way."

If you've trusted God with your life and dreams, and if you're continuing to look to Him for help, the Bible makes a pretty awesome promise: *"Whether you turn to the right or to the left, your ears will hear a voice behind you, saying, 'This is the way; walk in it'"* (Isaiah 30:21). That's the still, small voice of God's Spirit giving you guidance for your life. So don't just stand around waiting. Start walking and trust God to guide you all the way to where you need to go.

The true measure is what you and God can do together.

NEVER TOO YOUNG

So I think I've got this. I'm supposed to catch God's wave for my life. Go with the flow. Pray all the time. Follow the dream. But right now I'm just dreaming of understanding what in the world my science teacher is talking about. Oh, and dreaming of lunch. And cute guys or girls.

Ever feel like you're too young for all this? Too young to follow God's leading for your life? Or maybe you'd rather just put it all off until later. Think back on the stories you've read about kids and teens throughout this book. Remember Lauren and Lesley Reavely who started H20 to meet the physical and spiritual needs of homeless people? Don't forget Zach Hunter and his LC2LC, fighting to end slavery. Abby Sunderland dreamed of being the youngest person to sail around the world, and she went for it. Remember Cheyenne Little, who overcame her disability to work at the YMCA? And Joshua Guthrie, who is challenging fellow teens to give a dollar for a drink to provide clean water for others? Of course, there's always Bethany Hamilton coming all the way back to become a pro surfer and to tell the world about God's love. None of these teens let age stop them.

God wants you regardless of your age. He has plans for your life. He knows how old you are, and He knows how much you can or can't handle. That doesn't mean you *have* to have your life's dreams completely figured out by now. It just means age doesn't limit what God can use you to do. The true measure is what you and God can do together.

The Bible says, *"Don't let anyone look down on you because you are young, but set an example for the believers in speech, in life, in love, in faith and in purity"* (1 Timothy 4:12). As you ride God's wave, you can inspire other people. You can help them make their comeback. You can reach big dreams.

You may have a big dream already. Or you may be just starting to get an idea. Either way, now is the time to dive in and go with God's flow. He wants to lead you and guide you and make sure you're in the right place at the right time. You can trust Him. He loves you more than you know.

YOUR RIDE

Rewrite Proverbs 3:5–6, below, in the form of a prayer from you to God, asking Him to help you go with the flow and follow His lead.

Trust in the LORD with all your heart and lean not on your own understanding; in all your ways submit to him, and he will make your paths straight.

"Many things will catch your eye, but only a few will catch your heart ... Pursue those."
—Michael Nolan, author

"When we are rightly related to God, life is full of spontaneous, joyful uncertainty and expectancy— we do not know what God is going to do next; he packs our life with surprises."
—Oswald Chambers, author

"The more we receive in silent prayer, the more we can give in our active life."
—Mother Teresa

CHAPTER 22

DEEP AND WIDE

"Love. Bigger than any tidal wave. More powerful than any fear."

–Bethany Hamilton in the movie SOUL SURFER

In the movie SOUL SURFER, *when Bethany sees the people in the Thai village begin venturing back into the ocean, she realizes what is really important in life. It's not surfing. It's not winning trophies. It's not being sponsored by Rip Curl (although she got some pretty cool stuff). It's love. And even though Bethany has a wonderful family and some really loyal, encouraging friends, no one can love her as much as God.*

God IS love, and He is the ultimate source of love for each one of us. We know from the Bible that God loved us so much that He sent His Son, Jesus, to die for us! Now, that's definitely more powerful than any tidal wave. Read on to find out more about God's wide, deep, powerful love (for you)!

Karol Meyer experiences the ocean like practically no one else in the world. She's almost like a sea creature herself as she free dives to astounding depths. Free diving is way different than scuba diving because it doesn't use oxygen tanks. Free divers just hold their breath and regulate their bodies to the depth naturally. When Karol breathes pure oxygen first, she can hold her breath more than eighteen minutes straight without taking a breath! Seriously! You didn't read that wrong. Try holding your breath; you'd be doing good to hold it one minute.

God's love is even wider and deeper than the ocean—infinitely wider and deeper!

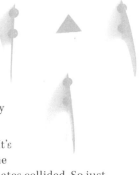

Karol discovered she had this skill when she was experimenting in a pool with friends and found out she could hold her breath for four minutes. After that, Karol started researching free diving, and she found her passion. Next came dreams of world records, and Karol claimed seven of them. In 2010, she made it 397 feet deep in a tandem dive with Patrick Musimu. Most humans would die before they got close to 397 feet. But Karol knows the power and depth of the ocean in a way many of us can't imagine. Still, her deepest dive barely breaks the surface of the ocean itself.

The deepest point on earth is the Mariana Trench. It's like a big canyon, 35,839 feet deep, at the bottom of the Pacific Ocean. It got there when some of the earth's plates collided. So just how deep is that? For reference, the highest point of land on earth above sea level is Mount Everest at a mere 29,035 feet. And most commercial airplanes fly at about 35,000 feet above the surface of the earth. So the Mariana Trench is deeper than the height you ride in an airplane.

Back in 1960, Jacques Piccard and Navy Lieutenant Donald Walsh descended in a bathyscaphe, basically a deep-water submarine-type vehicle, all the way down to 35,810 feet to check out the deepest spot on earth. They're the only humans to go that deep. In fact, the Mariana Trench is so deep that only two other robotic expeditions have dived down to explore it.

A lot of the ocean is a mystery to us because it's never been explored. There's just so much water on our planet, we don't understand it all. Check out these amazing ocean facts:

- Water covers 71 percent of the earth. Oceans contain 97 percent of that water.

- Of all life on the earth, 80 percent is found under the ocean's surface.

- Sound travels five times faster in water than air.

CATCHING GOD'S WAVE FOR YOUR LIFE

- Ocean tides are caused by the earth rotating while the gravitational pulls of the moon and sun act on ocean water.
- Earth's longest mountain range is the underwater Mid-Ocean Ridge. It's more than thirty-one thousand miles long, and it winds around the globe from the Arctic Ocean to the Atlantic, skirting Africa, Asia, and Australia, and crossing the Pacific to the west coast of North America. It's four times longer than the Andes, Rockies, and Himalayas combined.
- The oceans contain 99 percent of the living space on the planet, but less than 10 percent of it has been explored by humans.

We can hardly imagine the depth and power of the ocean. It can blow our minds if we really try to think about it. But try to wrap your mind around this: God's love is even wider and deeper than the ocean—infinitely wider and deeper! The power of the oceans can't begin to compare with God's. His power is way, way greater. The Bible says, *"Mightier than the thunder of the great waters, mightier than the breakers of the sea—the LORD on high is mighty"* (Psalm 93:4). That's why we can put our hope in Him.

We've talked a lot about our part in the process of becoming a soul surfer. That's important. But we can't ever forget that we can't do it alone. We *need* God.

He's the One who invites us to trust Him, to ride His wave, and to let Him take us through the adventures of our lives. Sometimes, we need a good reminder that on the waves of life, we can keep looking to Him as our source for everything. You name it, God is our beginning and end because He has no beginning or end. At some point, we all run out of help, hope, strength, and love—but God never does. God's love goes deeper and wider than all the oceans of the earth combined. You can never reach the end of God's love for you.

THE DEEPEST LOVE

The world loves a great love story—*Romeo and Juliet. West Side Story. Lady and the Tramp. Beauty and the Beast.* Pick your favorite. But the greatest love story of all is the one about the baby born in Bethlehem who sacrificed His life because of God's deep love for the whole world.

The Bible says, *"God loved the world so much that he gave his one and only Son, so that everyone who believes in him will not perish but have eternal life"* (John 3:16, NLT). That's some seriously sacrificial love. God loved you so much that He didn't want you to be separated from Him by sin. So He sent His only Son in the form of a human baby to grow up to be a man. He was betrayed and killed on the cross and then arose from the dead. God's love is so powerful that nothing, not even sin and death, could keep Him from gathering us back to Him. He would not be denied His children. He would not be satisfied until He had opened the way for each one to be restored to Him. He loves you. He cherishes you. And with all His heart, He wants you to take His hand and let Him lovingly guide and direct you along the path of your life.

Our love songs often talk about climbing the highest mountains and crossing the widest seas. God actually did that and more—way more. His love for you is deeper than you can ever fully grasp. It's wider than you can imagine. It goes higher and farther than the universe. And unlike human love, it's perfect.

The Bible contains the perfect description of love. It's modeled after the perfect love God has for each of us. *"Love is patient, love is kind. It does not envy, it does not boast, it is not proud. It is not rude, it is not self-seeking, it is not easily angered, it keeps no record of wrongs. Love does not delight in evil but rejoices with the truth. It always protects, always trusts, always hopes, always perseveres. Love never fails"* (1 Corinthians 13:4–8).

So what does it mean for you? It means that God's love welcomes you in. It means Jesus' arms spread wide on the cross are open wider than the sea to embrace you if you're willing to run into them and believe. It means you can spend your life exploring the depths of God's love. He wants you to dive into it, swim in it, splash in it, and discover new pools every day. You'll never totally understand it, but you can spend a lifetime enjoying it. And as you do, God's love will wash over you and transform you.

You can never reach the end of God's love for you.

The Bible says, *"May you have the power to understand, as all God's people should, how wide, how long, how high, and how deep his love is. May you experience the love of Christ, though it is too great to understand fully. Then you will be made*

And when our hope is in the depth of God's unchanging love, we will not be disappointed

complete with all the fullness of life and power that comes from God" (Ephesians 3:18–19 NLT). Wow! God loves you! No message is more important for you to hear than that. No message is more important for you to believe and embrace.

Now that we've learned some things about love, let's talk about hope.

HOPE

College is known for being fun. It is, but the reality is that it's also filled with pressure from exams, high tuition, trying to fit in on big campuses, and worries about jobs looming in the real world after graduation. There's still hope, though, just in a different form than you might expect. At Purdue University, "the compliment guys" are making sure of it.

Cameron Brown and Brett Westcott decided to try to raise people's spirits on their campus. For an entire year, the two friends stood on a sidewalk in the middle of Purdue with a "Free Compliments" sign and said something nice about every person who walked by. That's right, *every* single person.

So what kinds of things did they say? "Hey, I like that brown hoodie." "Enjoy the rest of that phone call, and tell that person to have a great day!" "Looking good today, sir. I like that hat!" "You guys are a very cute couple." "You've got really great curly hair." "Sir, you have a very luscious full coat of fur"—that one was to a dog.

People were skeptical at first, thinking Cameron and Brett were doing a sociology project or trying to pick up girls. But when they showed up every Wednesday—sun, rain, sleet, or snow—to say nice things, people began to appreciate it. Many students even planned their day around walking by the guys to hear a kind word. While they've been featured in news stories and even on *Good Morning America,* Cameron and Brett still stand by the fact that their real fulfillment was in bringing hope and encouragement to people who need a bright spot in their day.

The compliment guys are great! But did you know you have an even bigger fan who builds you up better than any compliment on earth? The Bible says, *"The LORD's delight is in those who fear him, those who put their hope in his unfailing love"* (Psalm 147:11, NLT). That's more than enough to make your day. God *delights* in you. He doesn't just put up with you or think you're okay most of the time. *Delight* means He takes pleasure in you, is glad about you, and is satisfied and happy about you. He wants you to feel the same about Him by putting your hope in His unfailing love, no matter what your life looks like right now.

God wants to show you that when you feel hopeless, there is hope—true hope. It's not based on your current situation but on God's eternal reality. Hope gives us something to look forward to. Hope isn't just wishful thinking like, "I hope I'll get a million dollars for my birthday." Hope is expecting that good will happen. It's like a fire inside that keeps burning even when things aren't looking so great. Hope keeps us going no matter what obstacles are in front of us.

In the movies, hope drives Marlin and Dory onward to find Nemo. Hope keeps Luke Skywalker fighting the Empire. Hope brings Mary Poppins to Jane and Michael as a nanny. Hope keeps Frodo and Sam traveling always toward Mount Doom.

In real life, hope in God doesn't disappoint. Hope drives us toward our dreams and expects God to work in big ways. It's what inspires and enables the whole adventure from the birth and discovery of our dreams, through the challenges and obstacles, and on to the accomplishments and fulfillments. The Bible tells us that the whole process of enduring and persevering through our obstacles and problems builds hope inside us—hope that something better is coming from God. And when our hope is in the depth of God's unchanging love, we will

God delights in you. He doesn't just put up with you or think you're okay most of the time.

not be disappointed (Romans 5:3–5). Really, hope is at the heart of being a soul surfer.

So plunge into God's wave for your life and ride on in His amazing love. Let Him fill you with unexplainable hope. And *"may the God of hope fill you with all joy and peace as you trust in him, so that you may overflow with hope by the power of the Holy Spirit"* (Romans 15:13).

YOUR RIDE

Make a heart for yourself as a reminder of God's love. Don't worry, guys, you don't have to use lace and ribbons; wire and wood work just as well. Of course, you could also use a paper clip, aluminum foil, clay, paper, or fabric. Be creative. You might want to add a favorite Bible verse. You might want it big to hang in your locker or bedroom or make it small to carry in your pocket or purse. No matter what your heart looks like, let it remind you that God really loves you. Let it give you hope whenever you see it.

"What does love look like? It has the hands to help others. It has the feet to hasten to the poor and needy. It has eyes to see misery and want. It has the ears to hear the sighs and sorrows of men. That is what love looks like."
—St. Augustine, philosopher

"Though our feelings come and go, God's love for us does not."
—C.S. Lewis

"God's love is measureless. It is more: It is boundless."
—A. W. Tozer

"God does not love us because we are valuable. We are valuable because God loves us."
—Archbishop Fulton J. Sheen

CHAPTER 23

WALKING ON WATER

"I wouldn't change what happened to me because then I wouldn't have this chance, in front of all of you, to embrace more people than I ever could with two arms."

–Bethany Hamilton in the movie SOUL SURFER

In the movie SOUL SURFER, when Bethany finishes in fifth place in the big surfing competition, she is quickly surrounded by a group of reporters who all want to know how she feels about her performance. Then a reporter asks a really tough question: "If you could go back to that day and not go surfing, would you do it?" How do you think most people would answer that? Would their answer be something like, "Dude, I would totally change what happened, are you kidding?" But that's not what Bethany says. Instead, she sees past the pain and the obstacles, and she realizes God has actually offered her the ride of her life. Her faith and her story are changing the world!

Have you ever wanted a life that was extraordinary? Amazing? Radical? Then maybe you know what we mean when we talk about walking on water. It's the idea that you can do something that seems impossible. If you like the thought of living that way, read on. In this chapter, you're going to meet some people whose lives are way beyond ordinary!

"What would you do if you had five minutes with a world leader?" That was the question Bob Goff asked his kids. His seven-year-old son said he'd ask the leader to come over for a sleepover. His nine-year-old son said he would ask the leader what he was hoping for, because maybe they would be hoping for the same thing. And his daughter said she would ask if she could go to the leader's house to film an interview.

So the Goff family wrote letters to leaders all over the world inviting them to a sleepover and promising that if they couldn't come over, the Goffs would fly to them to do the interview. They got lots of letters back, but they all said no. Finally, the president of Bulgaria answered, "If you come to the palace, I'll give you your interview."

Yes! The Goffs went to Bulgaria and interviewed the president. Eventually, they went to twenty-nine different countries and met with world leaders. Some of the things they saw while traveling prompted them to help kids their ages who were being forced into slavery. So Bob, who was a lawyer, founded Restore International to help bring justice and freedom to kids. But it all started with the wild and crazy ideas of three kids who weren't afraid to dream big.

Bob and his family are soul surfers embracing God's wave for their lives. When our hope is in the God of the universe, we can dream big too—really big, extravagantly big. Why? Because our soul-surfing journey is not about what we can do, it's about what God can do through us. As we ride God's wave forward in faith, there's no limit to what we can accomplish with Him.

Our soul-surfing journey is not about what we can do, it's about what God can do through us.

GET OUT OF THE BOAT

A lot of Jesus' disciples were fishermen. They knew the sea, ships, and how and where to catch the fish. It was what they did. It was their comfort zone.

One day, Jesus sent his guys across the Sea of Galilee. He was going to spend some time praying and then catch up with them later. None of them expected the kind of reunion they would have. The wind kicked up fast while the disciples were out in the middle of the sea. It was giving the experienced seamen all they could handle, as they fought

God wants us to dream so big that we have to trust and rely on Him.

to keep control of their boat in the wind and chaotic waves.

That's when they saw it, or Him. They weren't sure what it was. Something ... no, *someone* was coming toward them—walking on the water. They were freaked out. Those big, burly fishermen were screaming like little kids, "Ahhhh! It's a ghost!"

But—you know this part, right?—it was Jesus. He called out to them and told them not to be afraid.

Have you ever been at sea when it gets really windy? It's loud. Wind blows sea spray every which direction and makes the waves rise and fall unpredictably. Water slams down and sloshes from all sides. The disciples' wooden boat was probably creaking and groaning. Jesus' men heard Him call, but they still weren't totally convinced in the middle of all the chaos.

Peter was always the first of the guys to jump into something, often without thinking, but hey, he was usually willing to go for it. At any rate, he was bold enough to test things out. He shouted toward Jesus, *"Lord, if it's really you, tell me to come to you, walking on the water"* (Matthew 14:28 NLT).

"Come on," Jesus answered, and Peter stepped right out of the boat. He didn't hesitate. He went for it. And he discovered he was in the middle of a miracle. Peter didn't sink! He was walking—on the water! How many times had he been on this sea during his life? Too many to count. And every time he went over the edge of the boat, Peter went into the water and got wet. It's the way the world worked. But this time was different. There was a power working that was stronger than the laws of nature. Peter was walking on the water toward Jesus!

Peter couldn't believe it. Wait a minute ... he really couldn't believe it. This wasn't supposed to happen. *Oh no! The wind! This can't really be happening! What was I thinking? I wasn't thinking! I'm going to drown! Ahhhh!* Now he was sinking. "Save me, Lord!" he shouted.

Suddenly, Jesus was right there pulling Peter up and helping him back to the boat. "Why did you doubt me?" Jesus asked. In other words, "What happened? You were doing so good, Peter. Why did you start to doubt?"

Once the two were back in the boat, the wind stopped. Gone. Done. Jesus got rid of it with no problem. The disciples were wide-eyed. Their minds were truly blown. *"You really are the Son of God!' they exclaimed"* (Matthew 14:33 NLT). Whatever they thought they believed about Jesus before just went even deeper, and all they could do was worship Him.

You've got to wonder if some of the other disciples didn't think, *Man, I could have walked on water too! Why didn't I get up and go?* See, Jesus would have welcomed all the disciples in the boat if they had asked to step out and come to Him on the waves. That's His kind of dream. He's not limited by storms or problems or other people or anything that says, "You can't."

God wants us to dream so big that we have to trust and rely on Him. He wants us to imagine passing our own limitations. He wants us to go for a God sized dream. He's the God of the impossible, and He wants to prove it to us and use us to prove it to others. He wants to place ginormous dreams in our hearts and call us to walk on the waves toward Him. He wants to call us to do the impossible. Why? Because that calls us to Himself, and the impossible is only possible with God.

That's what Peter found out, and he gives us a reminder of how to pull off the impossible. We have to give big kudos to Peter for jumping out of the boat. At that point, all he saw was Jesus, and he was going for Him through the impossible. The wind, the sea, the law of gravity, none of that mattered. As long as Peter stayed focused on Jesus, he experienced the "impossible" and miraculous.

The problem came when Peter started focusing on everything else: the wind, the problems, the risks, the potential for failure, and the fact that he *shouldn't* be able to do what he was doing. Peter took his eyes off Jesus. That's when he sank.

Peter's a good reminder that we need to keep our eyes focused on Jesus, the ultimate soul surfer, as we ride God's wave for our lives. That's the most important thing. All our obstacles, pain, and discouragement don't have to bring us down. Jesus wants to keep us surfing over and through the wind and waves in our lives toward His impossible-made possible dreams. And He'll stay with us. He'll carry us through. He's there to steady us and grab us just like He grabbed Peter. But even more, He wants to help us believe. He wants to show us all that's possible.

See, the more impossible the dream, the clearer it becomes that God is the One making it happen. And when we see God working like that, it pumps up our confidence and makes our faith stronger. It gives us courage and hope. It inspires us to keep going. It also makes our lives an example to others of what God can do. It's like living a miracle.

DREAM IMPOSSIBLY BIG

Who do you know who is dreaming big? Who is walking on water? They don't have to be anywhere near water. You don't either. Walking on water is any dream God calls us to that can't be accomplished by our own strength and power. It's the stuff that's only possible with Him.

Sloan Henderson's dream is impossibly big. When she was twelve, she was really into horses. But when she broke her jaw in an accident, her dad hoped she would get into something a little safer. So much for that wish! Sloan started racing cars—and winning! Since then, she's been winning races and setting track records. In 2009, at seventeen, Sloan was the highest-ranked NASCAR female rookie! And she's not stopping there. Her team of family and friends and her faith in God are helping her continue to dream big. Sloan's goal? To be the first woman to win the NASCAR Sprint Cup Series. Her dream doesn't look quite so impossible now, does it?

Sometimes, dreaming big includes having big dreams for other people. When we dare to walk on water, we help other people discover they can walk on water too—even those who can barely stand. The Dream Center in Los Angeles, California, is helping people dream impossible dreams everyday. Actually, it's doing the impossible by showing people crushed by life that it's possible to dream again and reach their dreams.

There's no age requirement for walking on water. With God all things—and all ages—are possible!

"Find a need and fill it; find a hurt and heal it." That's the motto of the Dream Center. It sounds like an understatement when you look at what this church-based organization is doing. The Dream Center provides

Put your hand in His and let Him give you the power you need to keep walking on water.

opportunities and resources for people facing poverty, homelessness, and hopelessness. It provides food, clothing, shelter, life rehabilitation, education and job training, medical care, biblical training, and much more. And the Dream Center never closes. Its doors are open to anyone who needs assistance, twenty-four hours a day, 365 days a year. It has 273 ministries and outreaches that reach thousands every week. That's a lot of dreams for a lot of people. It's hope for the hopeless. The Dream Center's dreams are impossibly big for the inner city—but they're walking on water and watching God make them come true.

Sometimes, walking on water means doing your very best and then some. Sometimes, it means helping a kid in your class. Sometimes, it means reaching out globally. It happens through relationships and by starting with small steps—small, possible steps that lead to the impossible.

Chelsea Baker was a thirteen-year-old girl who was honored in the National Baseball Hall of Fame and Museum for pitching two perfect games—against boys. Lexi Allen was a sixteen-year-old artist who used her talents to start Art for Niños, which provides art supplies for poor kids in Latin America. And Maddy Beckmann was sixteen when she turned her compassion into Coat-a-Kid, an organization that gives donated winter gear to kids who don't have any. Eighteen-year-old Michael Sessions won the election and became the mayor of Hillsdale, Illinois, in 2005. Brittany McComb became valedictorian of her class and thanked Jesus in her graduation speech, even when her school told her she couldn't talk about God.

Normal teens aren't supposed to be able to do stuff like that, right? Says who? There's no age requirement for walking on water. With God all things—and all ages—are possible!

What is God calling you to? What's your impossible dream? Does it seem too big for you? Look, Jesus is calling to you. Take a step out of the boat and walk on the water. Trust in Jesus' promise that *"what is impossible for people is possible with God"* (Luke 18:27 NLT). He wants to prove it to you. Will you let Him?

REACH UP

Impossible can sound scary. It can look frightening. And we can all feel intimidated sometimes. That's okay. Remember the chapter about courage? Being bold and courageous doesn't mean you won't be scared. It means you keep going anyway. You don't let your fear stop you from stepping out of the boat.

The best thing you can ever remember no matter how much your knees are knocking is that Jesus is there. He understands your weaknesses and limitations. Yes, He wants to take you past them, but never alone. He always stays with you, and when you start to sink, His hand is there to hold you up and pull you out of the waves. He'll never let you down. When you feel yourself falling, reach up. Put your hand in His and let Him give you the power you need to keep walking on water.

YOUR RIDE

This is a dream-o-meter. You know, kind of like the old-timey love-o-meter you might have seen at an arcade or amusement park. Think of three dreams. Place them where you think they fall on the scale of dreaming big. How'd you do? Is there a dream you can add to the top level, like walking on water?

Walking on Water!

Peering Over the Side of the Boat

Reaching New Heights

Achieving

Taking Baby Steps, Every Day

Barely Making It Out of Bed

Dream, What Dream?

_____

_____

_____

"If I had asked people what they wanted, they would have said faster horses."

—Henry Ford, industrialist

"Dreams come a size too big so that we can grow into them."

—Josie Bissett, actress

"If you can dream it, you can do it."

—Walt Disney, founder-creator of the Walt Disney Company

CHAPTER 24

IT ALL COUNTS

"I didn't come to win. I came to surf."

–Bethany Hamilton in the movie SOUL SURFER

In the movie SOUL SURFER, it looks like Bethany is going to pull off an amazing feat and win the Rip Curl National Surfing Competition, riding in the barrel of the biggest wave of the contest. But because she dropped into the wave after the horn sounded, her score doesn't count. Afterward, a reporter asks her if she's upset that she didn't win. Winning is a matter of perspective though, and Bethany totally gets that. The wave counted to Bethany because what really matters are the two things she loves the most—surfing and following God.

That's the kind of answer you expect from a soul surfer. What counts is living a life that makes a difference as you use your gifts and do what you love best. Are you ready to finish up this book and get going on your own soul-surfing adventure? Well, read on ... you're almost there!

Bethany Hamilton's comeback was big—impossibly big. After losing her arm to the shark, she was back surfing again just a short while later. She was competing again—and making the regional finals—within another couple of months. Bethany charged back and made the impossible possible so fast that it almost looked easy. But it wasn't at all.

Every step took courage, persistence, and faith. In one of her first competitions, Bethany struggled to match the strength and skill of the other surfers. All the girls were good. Plus, they had both arms to paddle and maneuver with to catch the waves. Bethany was still getting used to doing everything with one arm. She was trailing her rival, time was running out, and the ocean had gone flat. There were no waves in sight. The girls sat and waited hoping for a swell to appear on the horizon, hoping for another wave to ride. Would it come in time?

Bethany stared hard toward the horizon, watching, waiting, and sensing the energy of the ocean around her. Then she began to paddle farther out and away from the other surfers, away from where the waves had been breaking all day. Then, there was a bump on the water's surface far out at sea: a swell rolling in, a big one, the biggest of the day. And Bethany was there to catch it. It was a beautiful wave that churned out a perfect, hollow barrel. Bethany surfed deep inside its sparkling tube of water for a perfect ride. It was by far the best ride of the day, and the score should have put her in first place for the win.

But the competition clock had run out—the last wave didn't count. Bethany didn't win. When Bethany reached the beach, she was met with frustration and disappointment from her friends and family. They argued that her wave should have counted. They were ready to protest to the judges. But Bethany was all smiles and uncontainable joy. "It counted. It totally counted," she told her dad.

No, the wave didn't count for the competition, but it counted for Bethany. It counted in the much-bigger picture, and Bethany knew it. It counted for Jesus, whom she was following. You see, Bethany is a soul surfer. She gives her all to compete and win and to do the best she can, but she surfs for much more than points, wins, and titles. It didn't matter that Bethany's perfect wave didn't win her the contest. It was a ginormous step in her comeback and in her life's journey. She knew her dream was alive.

WHAT COUNTS?

Who are you surfing for? Where are you on your journey? How are you counting your success? God counts every wave. When we're soul surfing with Him, it doesn't matter if the world gives us big credit for what we're doing.

This book is full of stories of people who have received attention for what they've done or are doing. They're inspirational. They deserve recognition. But most of us faithfully pursuing our dreams and passions will never make it into a book or on the news. However, all of us will get even bigger and better props—from God! He sees. He knows. The Bible tells us He knows everything about us and what we do. There's nothing He misses. And He counts every wave. He's with us every single step: the good and bad ones, the hard and easy ones, the ones that feel like failures, and the ones that are great victories. His opinion counts most.

Sometimes, it just takes other people a while to catch up or catch on, especially if your dream redefines what's possible. Remember Galileo? He was the famous scientist, mathematician, and astronomer who made amazing discoveries and contributed valuable information to the world back in the Middle Ages. He's been called the father of modern science. But back in the day, Galileo didn't receive lots of praise and awards. Instead, he got rejection. What he saw was possible and what he discovered was true, but no one believed him then. He said the earth revolved around the sun, but people didn't want to hear it. Worse, he was accused of heresy and arrested for his scientific claims. It was only after his death, when other scientists continued to prove his theories, that Galileo became a hero. He didn't live to see his dream recognized, but it all counted! His work was not in vain.

Every step you take in your journey of living life with God counts whether you're noticed and appreciated or not. It counts whether you see the end result or not. It counts in God's big picture, and it counts because He uses it to shape you into the person He has made you to be. It's okay if the world doesn't stand up and cheer—God is with you, watching and guiding you every step of the way. He's the cheering part that matters. When the world tries to knock you down, listen for God's voice. Get up and keep following His lead onto the next wave. Let God fill you with His inspiration and encouragement whether you receive a lot of praise from people or none at all.

Whatever your unique calling is, wherever you are in the process of discovering and pursuing it, you can count on the fact that God does have a plan for you.

BORN TO MAKE A DIFFERENCE

Think back to the beginning of this book. We talked about God as your Creator. He made you special and unique. You're a one-of-a-kind blend of genes, gifts, abilities, talents, and vision. You're full of potential and promise, and God has placed a dream in your heart. Your dream isn't static, stuck in one place. It's fluid, moving, developing, and changing as you learn, grow, and experience life. Right now, you might be dreaming of passing algebra or getting a certain girl or guy to notice you. Next year, you might be dreaming of being a doctor, a senator, or both. As God guides you forward on His wave for your life, He helps you learn and see new things.

But there's one fact that never changes: You were born to make a difference. Whatever your unique calling is, wherever you are in the process of discovering and pursuing it, you can count on the fact that God does have a plan for you. That plan makes a difference in the world. And every step you take along the way counts. It's all part of God's big picture for your life and the lives of those He'll touch through you.

Bethany's story doesn't count just because she found a way to surf again after a tragic accident. It continues to count because she continues to pursue her unique calling in life—not only to surf but to point to Jesus and help others catch God's wave for their lives. Living for that purpose has brought Bethany joy, peace, and fulfillment. Today, she's one of the top pro surfers in the world. She's recognized by people all over the world who remember the story of her shark attack. She's had the chance to tell millions about God's love and to show them His power working in her life.

No one expected that on Halloween morning. No one dreamed of it then. Bethany and her family had trouble imagining it as she lay recovering in a hospital room. But they began to hope. They took hold of God's promise, "*'I know the plans I have for you,' declares the LORD, 'plans to prosper you and not to harm you, plans to give you hope and a future'*" (Jeremiah 29:11). Then Bethany went for her dream with all her might. She never gave up. When people noticed, she pointed them toward Jesus and encouraged them to never give up.

That's good advice. Never give up. Go for it.

THE BEGINNING

Congratulations! You've reached the end—of the book, that is. But it's only the beginning for you. The great adventure of God's wave for your life lies in front of you, and He welcomes you to join Him on the adventure of a lifetime.

Maybe you're already on it. Maybe you're standing on the shore thinking about diving in. Maybe you're nowhere near the water. You might have a dream for your life. You might have some vague ideas. Or you might have absolutely no idea. Good, because in one sense it doesn't really matter. Wherever you are right now, God wants to take you deeper into His wave of love, grace, and power.

He wants to remind you where you've come from and where you're going. He wants you to know how special He created you to be and how much He loves you. He wants to fill you with passions, lead you into adventures, and reveal your gifts and dreams. God wants you to know you can trust Him even when you wipe out. He wants to heal you after a tumble in the impact zone and give you strength and courage to face your problems. He wants to help you overcome your challenges and fill you with love for other people. God wants to help you never give up. He wants to laugh with you in amazement as you walk on water. God wants you to come soul surfing with Him.

Open your arms and heart to Him. He'll send the wave—the most meaningful and exciting one around. You just have to say yes to catch it. Dive in!

YOUR RIDE

Flip back and move forward. Look over your notes and activities from the end of each chapter. Pick your favorite Bible verse and quote. Put it on your wall or make it your screen saver. Use these reminders to write down a few notes to yourself on this page.

What three action steps can you take now to live as a soul surfer?

"We must not, in trying to think about how we can make a big difference, ignore the small daily differences we can make which, over time, add up to big differences that we often cannot foresee."
—Marian Wright Edelman, founder and president of the Children's Defense Fund

"Life is a great big canvas, and you should throw all the paint on it you can."
—Danny Kaye, actor and singer

"Each day when I awake I know I have one more day to make a difference in someone's life."
—James Mann, American author

"Surfing isn't the most important thing in life. Love is. I've had the chance to embrace more people with one arm than I ever could with two."
—Bethany Hamilton, pro surfer

TIME FOR YOUR
SOUL-SURFING ADVENTURE

"Life is a lot like surfing. When you get caught in the impact zone, you need to get right back up, because you never know what's over the next wave. And if you have faith, anything is possible, anything at all."

—Bethany Hamilton in the movie SOUL SURFER

At the end of the movie SOUL SURFER, *we hear Bethany's inspiring words, and they remind us of some important truths. Yes, life IS a lot like surfing. You get knocked down, but it's important to get right back up and keep going. And with faith all things are possible.*

As we come to the end of this book, read these last few paragraphs about the role faith can play in your life.

Thanks for hanging with us to the end. You're still reading. That's good, because it probably means there's something inside your heart resonating with the sound of God's wave. That's the pull of His love calling you closer to Him. That's at the heart of what soul surfing is all about.

So now it's your turn to do something about it. Reading about soul surfing is a great start, but what will you do with the things you've learned in this book? And more important, what will you do with your life? How will you turn your inspiration into action? Don't stop listening to God's call to your heart. Let it go deep into your heart and change your life. Wherever you are in the process right now, ask God for the courage to take the next step. Ask Him for all you need to make soul surfing personal.

We've talked about it before, but the journey starts with the first step of trusting God with your life and receiving His grace to live as a soul surfer. Jesus wants a relationship with you—He wants to be your Lord and Savior. Now is the time to let Him. Tell Him you want that too. Admit that you need Him to forgive you and fill you with His Spirit. Accept the gift of eternal life that He made possible when He died on the cross for your sins. Commit to following Him with all your heart and soul. If you have more questions about what that means or looks like, talk with someone who knows Him. That could be the person who gave you this book, a friend, a parent, or a youth leader.

If you're already a follower of Jesus, ask for His help in riding His wave for your life. That goes for whether you've just given Him your life or you've known Him for years. Be honest with Him about your questions, confusions, hopes, and dreams. Ask Him to make you courageous in the pursuit of the dream He has placed in you. He wants you to dream big and change the world.

Dive into God's Word and get to know His ways. There are amazing things to discover in the Bible, and God's Spirit will bring it alive for you. Best of all, you'll find stories about Jesus and read the words He spoke in His time here on earth. He's your ultimate example and guide. He's the One who will show you what it means to live the exciting adventure of a relationship with God.

So dive in. Go deep. Swim in the ocean of God's love. Let His grace transform you into the person He created you to be. And when you feel the wave rising, don't hold back. Paddle with all your might and have the courage to stand. You, our soul-surfing friend, are in for the ride of your life!

ABOUT THE AUTHORS

Jeremy and Janna Jones are award-winning writers and editors who have written a wide variety of books and magazine articles. The couple wrote the book *Toward the Goal: The Kaká Story*, the biography of Brazilian soccer star Kaká. Jeremy's other books include *Walking on Water: The Spirituality of the World's Top Surfers* and the soon-to-be-released devotionals *Triple Dog Dare* and *The One Year Sports Devos for Kids*.

Earlier in their careers, Jeremy and Janna were both editors of teen magazines. Jeremy served as senior associate editor of *Breakaway*, and Janna was managing editor of *Go!* Now you can read their articles in magazines including *Transworld Snowboarding, Sports Spectrum, Christianity Today, Susie, Clubhouse, Clubhouse Jr.*, and others.

You might think these two met at a library or publishing convention—but they actually met while working at a dude ranch. The Joneses currently spend lots of time trying to keep up with their two young children and two old dogs. They love road trips and exploring the mountains around their home in Colorado.

SOUL SURFER DVD-based Study
Be inspired by this four-week study featuring exclusive video of Bethany Hamilton.

This four-week DVD-based study includes a resource DVD with *Heart of a Soul Surfer*—a thirty-minute documentary with interviews—and exclusive surfing and family footage of Bethany Hamilton before and after the shark attack. *Heart of a Soul Surfer* digs deep into the heart of Bethany's unwavering faith in God and provides video clips to support the four-week study.

With its encouraging portrayal of family values and its uplifting message, the *SOUL SURFER* DVD-based Study will resonate with adults, families, and teens alike!

The kit includes:

· *Heart of a Soul Surfer* documentary plus clips for four weekly lessons

· A *SOUL SURFER* Study Guide

· A leader's guide with instructions for small group leaders, parents, and youth leaders

Heart of a Soul Surfer
The powerful, inspirational story of Bethany Hamilton on DVD!

Special Edition DVD includes:

- Widescreen Format
- Subtitles in 9 Languages
- New Bonus Videos
  "Day in the Life"
  "Surf Training with Bethany"
  "Gospel Presentation"
- Free 13 x 9 Poster of Bethany

Heart of a Soul Surfer: The Bethany Hamilton Documentary offers her family's perspective on the true story and life of a promising young surfer who discovered her purpose in life as she overcame the loss of her arm to a fourteen-foot tiger shark in 2003.

This thirty-minute, faith-based documentary conveys Bethany's heart and tackles the difficult question, Why does God allow bad things to happen in our lives? Dealing with topics from self-consciousness to courage to faith in God, *Heart of a Soul Surfer* presents an inspiring story and message in a fun, exciting way— told from the heart of a young woman with great passion and dedication to God.